SMART MONEY FAITHFUL LIVING

Faith, Wisdom, and Strategies for Financial Stability

GODIBERTHE MUTAYISEBYA

Licensed Financial Professional

Copyright © 2025 Godiberthe Mutayisebya
All Rights Reserved
No part of this publication may be reproduced or distributed in any form or by any means without the prior permission of the author and/or publisher.

152 -160 City Road, London, EC1V 2NX, United Kingdom

ISBN: 978-1-917451-58-1

Published by Action Wealth Publishing and Godiberthe Mutayisebya
Printed in the United Kingdom

Scripture quotations taken from The Holy Bible, New International Version® NIV® Copyright © 1973, 1978, 1984, 2011 by Biblica, Inc.® Used with permission. All rights reserved worldwide.

Scripture quotations from the ESV® Bible (The Holy Bible, English Standard Version®), copyright© 2001 by Crossway Bibles, a publishing ministry of Good News Publishers. Used by permission. All rights reserved.

Additional scripture quotations from the King James version (KJV) of the Bible, in the public domain.

Although the author and publisher have made every effort to ensure the accuracy and completeness of information contained in this book, we assume no responsibility for errors, inaccuracies, omissions, or any inconsistency herein. Any slights on people, places, or organisations are unintentional. The material in this book is provided for educational purposes only. No responsibility for loss occasioned to any person or corporate body acting or refraining to act as a result of reading material in this book can be accepted by the author or publisher.

"True wealth isn't measured by what you have, but by how faithfully you steward what you've been given."

—Godiberthe M.

This book is lovingly dedicated to my mother, whose quiet wisdom, unwavering faith, and everyday sacrifices taught me the true meaning of stewardship.

She showed me that smart money isn't just about numbers; it's about discipline, dignity, and doing the right thing when no one is watching, integrity. She lived faithfully, gave generously, and managed little with grace, often making much out of very little.

It was through her example that I first learned that managing money is a spiritual act, and that how we handle what we have reflects who we are and what we believe.

"A story well told can move hearts, shift mindsets, and shape legacies because sometimes the most valuable truth comes wrapped in a life well lived."

—Godiberthe M.

"You may have tangible wealth untold, Caskets of jewels and coffers of gold. Richer than I you can never be I had a mother who read to me."
— Strickland Gillilan

CONTENTS

ACKNOWLEDGMENTS 12
PREFACE 14
    Why Trust This Book? 15
    Your Invitation to Transformation 15
PART I: FOUNDATIONS OF FAITH AND FINANCE
.... 17
CHAPTER ONE: THE POWER OF FAITH IN FINANCIAL STABILITY 18
    Faith and Financial Success 19
    From Hope to Habit 20
    Faith vs. Fantasy 21
    When Faith Fuels Discipline 21
    Biblical Principles of Stewardship 22
    Stewardship in Daily Practice 23
    Multiplying What's in Your Hand 23
    Trusting God with My Finances 24
    Making Sound Decisions Under Pressure 25
    The Role of Faith in Financial Recovery 26
    Anchors of Trust 27
    Conclusion 30
CHAPTER TWO: MONEY AND MINDSET: BREAKING FINANCIAL LIMITING BELIEFS 33

When I Thought Money Was Out of My Control 34
Shifting My Mindset, Rewriting My Story 35
The Fear of Managing Money 36
From Victim to Steward 36
Breaking Free from the Scarcity Mindset 37
Faith Tested Through Financial Struggles 39
Working Against the Odds 39
When Faith Was My Only Resource 40
Wealth, Hard Work, and Self-Reliance on Scripture 41
Scripture on Self-Reliance and Diligence 42
The Balance Between Faith and Work 43
Conclusion 44

CHAPTER THREE: THE PRICE OF FINANCIAL IGNORANCE 46

Understanding the Impact of Childhood Experiences ... 47
The Messages I Absorbed Without Words 48
Repeating Patterns I Didn't Understand 49
Rewriting the Money Script 49
Healing Deep-rooted Emotional Wounds 50
From Self-doubt to Self-acceptance 52
Reclaiming Personal Power Embedded in Truth 53
Conclusion 55

CHAPTER FOUR: FINANCIAL DISCIPLINE AND DELAYED GRATIFICATION 57

The Power of Self-control in Finances 58
Biblical Wisdom on Self-control and Money 59
Needs vs. Wants 60

The Value of Waiting ... 61
Why Waiting Aligns with Faithful Living ... 63
The Long-Term Reward of Financial Discipline ... 63
Conclusion ... 65
Lessons From Part One: Foundations of Faith and Finance ... 66

PART II: SMART STRATEGIES FOR MONEY MANAGEMENT ... 68

CHAPTER FIVE: BUDGETING WITH PURPOSE ... 69
Recognising the Signs of Living in Survival Mode ... 70
Awareness of Survival-Mode Indicators ... 72
Shifting from Reactivity to Intentional Living ... 74
Practical Steps to Build Resilience ... 76
How to Thrive in Daily Life ... 79
Conclusion ... 80

CHAPTER SIX: THE DISCIPLINE OF SAVING ... 82
The Habit of Saving ... 82
Paying Yourself First ... 85
Think Beyond Today ... 95
Tools for Long-Term Financial Vision ... 99
Conclusion ... 111

CHAPTER SEVEN: ESCAPING THE DEBT TRAP ... 113
Considering the True Cost of Debt ... 113
Steps for Eliminating Debt ... 118
Cultural and Social Pressures That Lead to Debt ... 122
How to Resist Cultural and Social Pressures ... 127
Creating a Debt-Free Lifestyle ... 130

Conclusion..134
PART III: BUILDING WEALTH WITH WISDOM..136
CHAPTER EIGHT: CREATING MULTIPLE STREAMS
OF INCOME...137
Relying on One Source of Income is Risky...................138
Identify Your Skills and Income Opportunity................141
Making Money Work for You 143
Balancing Multiple Streams Without Burnout...............146
Conclusion..148
CHAPTER NINE: INVESTING FOR THE FUTURE...151
Investing is the Key to Long-Term Wealth....................152
The Different Types of Investment................................154
Overcome the Fear of Investing 157
Create an Investment Plan that Works for You.............160
Conclusion..164

CHAPTER TEN: FINANCIAL FREEDOM AND
GENEROSITY...167
Stop Letting Money Control You...................................168
Breaking the Emotional Ties..169
Redefining Success...170
Build Wealth with a Purpose 172
From Accumulation to Assignment................................174
Purpose as the Guardrail..176
Giving – The Secret to Lasting Wealth..........................178
Giving Unlocks a Cycle of Increase...............................180
Forms of Giving 182

Start Living Freely *NOW!* 185
Freedom in Mindset 186
A Legacy of Peace 189
Conclusion 191

PART IV: LEGACY BUILDING AND LONG-TERM PLANNING 194

CHAPTER ELEVEN: SECURING YOUR FAMILY'S FUTURE 195

Why Estate Planning and Life Insurance Matter 196
How to Create Long-term Financial Security 198
Start Protecting What Matters 201
Your Legacy Starts TODAY! 202
Conclusion 203

CHAPTER TWELVE: RAISING MONEY-SMART CHILDREN 205

If Not You, Someone Else Will 206
Other Influences That Shape Financial Beliefs 207
Money Lessons Begin at Home 208
How Children Can Practice What They Learn 209
Teach Financial Responsibility Instead of Handouts 212
Responsibilities Over Rewards 214
Teaching Through Consequences 215
Your Money Habits Become Theirs 215
Modelling Healthy Financial Rhythms 217
Normalise Financial Conversations 217
From Observation to Ownership 218
Conclusion 219

CHAPTER THIRTEEN: BECOME A FINANCIAL MENTOR AND EDUCATOR 221

Financial Literacy Should Be Shared, Not Kept 222
Demonstrate Financial Principles to Family, Friends, & Community 223
The Role of Faith-Based Financial Coaching 225
Mentorship and Coaching for Financial Success 226
Get in Touch: Become a Financial Leader and Mentor 227
Conclusion 230

CHAPTER FOURTEEN: TAKE CONTROL OF YOUR FINANCIAL FUTURE 232

Explore the Right Financial Protection for You 233
Join Our Financial Literacy Training Program 236
Attend Live Events and Financial Workshops 240
Sustain Wealth Beyond a Lifetime 241
Conclusion 242

CONCLUSION: YOUR NEXT STEP TO MAKING SMART-MONEY CHOICES 244

FINANCIAL COACHING & TRAINING ENROLMENT FORM 247

ABOUT THE AUTHOR 250

ACKNOWLEDGMENTS

To my mother: thank you for the lessons you lived more than the ones you spoke. This book is a tribute to your faithful living and a legacy I hope to pass on.

To my late father, Gerard Munyankuge, your love, gentleness, and generosity were remarkable, even though it was just for a few years. My late siblings, Gerardine and Deogratias, your memories will forever live on.

To those individuals who contributed to my education, my grandparents, aunts, and uncles, I will never forget your sacrifices and support. Adele Ayinkamiye, Jean Marie Vianey Rusingizandekwe, Louis Ndushabandi, Pastor Justin Kanamugire, Prof. Laurent Kajeguhakwa, your legacy lives on.

I would like to express my sincere gratitude to everyone who supported me throughout the process of writing and publishing this book.

I must express my profound appreciation to my husband, Dr. Josue Mpayamaguru, my children, Godlives, Godever and Godwins, and my sister Germaine Mukayiranga, whose relentless efforts and professional guidance were instrumental in bringing this project to fruition. Your expertise, teamwork, engagement and encouragement were indispensable. I cannot spell success without U.

To my extended family members, my Shiloh church family, and my friends, I am eternally grateful for your love and support.

To Mr. and Mrs. Semaganda and their entire team at Action Wealth Publishing, thank you for believing in me and allowing me to spring forth my potential and talents.

I have made an effort in this project. However, it would not have been possible without the kind support and help of many individuals. I want to extend my sincere thanks to all of them.

"Life is an exciting business, and most exciting when it is lived for others."

—Helen Keller

PREFACE

Money is more than currency. It reflects our values, discipline, and faith. How we earn, spend, and manage our finances can either set us on a path of stability or lead us into unnecessary struggles. Many people live in constant financial uncertainty, not because they lack income, but because they lack wisdom, the kind that turns financial opportunities into lasting security.

This book is not just about money management but about money stewardship, aligning wisdom and strategy to create financial stability, honour God, and secure the future. It is also about understanding that money is not the enemy, nor is it the ultimate goal. Rather, it is a tool that, when used wisely, can provide freedom, security, and a foundation for greater impact in the lives of those we love.

If you have ever wondered why financial peace seems out of reach despite your hard work, struggled with saving, debt, or financial planning, or been searching for a way to align your financial habits with your faith, then you are holding the right book. The truth is that financial success is not about luck or privilege but knowledge and discipline. Just as we prepare for spiritual growth through prayer and bible study, we must also prepare for financial growth through education and action.

Why Trust This Book?

The wisdom in these pages is rooted in experience, faith, and real-life application. I am an advocate for financial literacy and a living testament to the power of perseverance, discipline, and financial education. Raised in a home where financial hardship was a reality, I witnessed firsthand how resourcefulness, strategic planning, and faith-driven decision-making could shape a brighter future. From circumnavigating the challenges of funding education, working across different countries, and starting businesses to becoming a Licensed Financial Professional, I have spent years empowering families, small businesses, and individuals to take charge of their financial futures.

My teachings are about wealth creation, freedom from financial stress and debt, and living with purpose and generosity. In this book, I share my professional insights and the timeless biblical principles that have shaped my journey toward financial wisdom.

Your Invitation to Transformation

This book is not meant to be skimmed but to be experienced. Each chapter is crafted to educate, inspire, and challenge you to take action in your financial life. As you read, you will be equipped with practical strategies, strengthened by biblical wisdom, and encouraged by real-life experiences that demonstrate that financial freedom is not just a dream but a tangible reality.

So, I invite you to take this faithful step toward financial transformation. With an open heart and a willingness to learn, turn to Chapter One, and let's begin this journey to Smart Money Faithful Living, a life where financial stability and spiritual faithfulness walk hand in hand.

Let Us Get Started!

PART I

FOUNDATIONS OF FAITH AND FINANCE

CHAPTER ONE

THE POWER OF FAITH IN FINANCIAL STABILITY

"The plans of the diligent lead surely to abundance, but everyone who is hasty comes only to poverty."

– Proverbs 21:5 (ESV)

Before financial strategies, budgets, or savings goals can truly take root, we must first examine the beliefs and inner convictions that guide our financial behaviour. The power of faith in financial stability is not merely about religious devotion; it's about building a deep, inner confidence that tomorrow can be better than today. Faith forms the unseen foundation beneath every wise financial decision.

It gives us the courage to act, the patience to endure seasons of lack, and the motivation to manage our resources with care. Whether drawn from spiritual beliefs, personal values, or a vision for a better life, this kind of faith provides the strength to rise above fear, make intentional choices, and pursue financial well-being with clarity and purpose.

In the pages that follow, you'll see how this faith-inspired foundation unfolds through personal habits, wise distinctions, grounded trust, disciplined choices, and timeless lessons. Each section brings these values to life, not in theory but in practice, starting with how hope becomes a habit and ending with how lived experience shapes lifelong wisdom.

Faith and Financial Success

Financial stability is not a coincidence. It is the product of intentional choices, thoughtful planning, and, for many of us, a quiet but unshakable belief that our circumstances can and will improve. Faith, in this context, is not simply a religious principle; it is a powerful attitude. It is the belief that the future can be better than the present and that we have both the power and responsibility to make it so.

Faith does not eliminate the need for effort. Rather, it fuels it. When we believe that something greater is possible, we find the strength to take action. Financial success begins with a belief in our ability to earn, budget, save, invest, grow, and manage money wisely. This belief often emerges from deeply rooted values of trust in hard work, commitment to integrity, and confidence that our efforts, no matter how small, are not in vain.

Faith also teaches us patience. Many people want financial breakthroughs without embracing the process of discipline and sacrifice that leads there. Faith calls us to trust the process. It assures us that, with consistency, even modest steps can lead to significant change. Whether you call it faith in God, in growth, or your potential, it is the fuel that turns good intentions into tangible results.

From Hope to Habit

It is one thing to believe that financial stability is possible and another to develop the habits that make it happen. Faith often begins with a strong sense of hope, especially when circumstances look bleak. But if hope is not followed by habit, it remains a wish. What turns hope into progress is consistency in small decisions: preparing a budget, choosing to save rather than spend, and saying no when it's easier to say yes.

I've learned that it's not the big leaps but the daily routines that move you forward. The practice of reviewing my expenses, setting aside even the smallest amount for savings, or reevaluating my priorities these simple actions, repeated over time transformed hope into results. Becoming is a process. When your faith translates into discipline, even your smallest financial steps become sacred. Faith without action is dead.

Faith vs. Fantasy

There's a delicate line between believing in possibilities and escaping into fantasies. True faith acknowledges the reality of your current situation while believing in your ability to grow beyond it. Fantasy, on the other hand, shies away from the present and clings to vague wishes, hoping for miracles without making plans or taking action.

I've seen too many people confuse these two. They pray for breakthroughs but ignore their budget. They wish for more income but resist the discipline of learning new skills or cutting unnecessary expenses. Faith is not passive. It challenges you to work with what you have while believing in what you can build. Real financial success requires faith that is grounded in truth, not detached from it.

When Faith Fuels Discipline

Some of the strongest financial decisions I've made were not rooted in fear or obligation but in faith. I believed that I could do better, which pushed me to budget with purpose. It was faith in the value of stability that kept me from reckless spending. Every time I delayed gratification or chose long-term gain over short-term comfort, it was because I trusted in the bigger picture. It is said that when you know your WHY, you will figure out the HOW. My dream, my vision and my faith are manifested in my discipline.

Discipline is easier to sustain when it's tied to belief. You save because you believe your future matters. You invest because you trust the seeds you're planting will bear fruit. You stay consistent because you believe progress is possible, even if it's slow. Faith doesn't replace effort, but it gives your effort direction.

Biblical Principles of Stewardship

Stewardship is a principle that teaches us to manage what we have with care, accountability, and a purposeful approach. In biblical tradition, stewardship isn't just about tithing or giving; it is about how we handle everything entrusted to us, the 4Ts: our Time, Talents, Temple (our body) and, yes, Treasure (our money).

The idea is simple but powerful: nothing we have is truly ours to waste. Whether it is a paycheck, a business, or a small plot of land, we are expected to manage it wisely. The Bible speaks of the faithful steward who is found trustworthy with little and later trusted with much. That principle applies as strongly to money management today as it did centuries ago.

Financial stewardship is not about having more; it's about making the most of what you already have. It involves living within your means, planning for the future, avoiding unnecessary debt, and being generous without being careless. These are not just good ideas but rather proven strategies that lead to financial stability.

When stewardship becomes a lifestyle, it changes the way we make decisions. It teaches us that every coin has a purpose, every bill has a plan, and every opportunity to earn or save is a sacred responsibility.

Stewardship in Daily Practice

We often think of stewardship as something formal or grand. However, the truth is that stewardship is evident in our everyday choices. It's in how we handle our grocery shopping, buying what we need, storing it properly, and avoiding waste. It's in how we treat our time that we determine whether we're using it to grow or to distract ourselves.

Financial stewardship becomes a way of life when we start asking intentional questions: Do I need this, or do I want it? Am I managing what I already have before asking for more? Am I grateful for the resources I have today, even as I work toward better? Every financial decision, however small, reflects how seriously we take our role as stewards of our resources.

Multiplying What's in Your Hand

There's a principle I've seen time and again: when you honour what you already have, more tends to come. I recall seasons when I had only a single skill or a small opportunity, yet treating it with respect opened doors that I never imagined. It might be typing, tutoring, or helping someone manage their fellow students' paperwork, or manufacturing soymilk, but giving your best to that small thing is often the first step toward abundance.

We are not always given much to start with, but we are always given something. My professor in Management class defined entrepreneurship as creating something out of nothing. The question is, are we using it? Are we multiplying it? When I reflect on the path that led me to become a financial educator, it didn't start with wealth. It started with a simple decision to do what I could, with what I had, where I was.

Reflection Questions

⌘ *How has your belief system influenced the way you perceive and manage money?*

⌘ *Are you using your values as a compass in your financial life?*

Trusting God with My Finances

No one escapes financial challenges. Whether it's a job loss, a medical emergency, or simply not having enough to make ends meet, these seasons test more than our wallets; they test our mindset. It is during these times that trust becomes vital.

Trusting during financial uncertainty doesn't mean pretending everything is okay. It means choosing not to panic. It means recognising that struggle doesn't last forever, and that smart, steady action will carry us through. Trust enables us to respond rather than react. Instead of emotional spending or borrowing out of fear, trust anchors us in discipline. It reminds us that we've come through difficult times before, and we can do it again. "This too, shall pass."

Trust is also about listening. In moments of pressure, we are often guided toward wise decisions through quiet reflection or through the advice of someone we respect. Trust in the process gives us the courage to make difficult decisions, such as downscaling, starting anew, seeking help, or changing course entirely. "I am never afraid to start again. Restart is always better than regrets." One of the mentors put these words as a command: "Start late, start over, start scared, start unprepared, just start."

Making Sound Decisions Under Pressure

There are moments when the pressure is overwhelming, and the temptation to make impulsive financial choices feels justified, especially when bills are due, income is tight, or an emergency arises. I've lived those moments. However, I've learned that even under pressure, wisdom remains attainable. Trusting God doesn't mean avoiding decision-making; it means slowing down long enough to seek clarity before taking action.

In times of stress, I ask myself simple but grounding questions: *Is this choice aligned with my long-term goals? Am I reacting emotionally or responding wisely?* Most importantly, I pray not as a last resort but as a first response. Even a few minutes of quiet reflection can shift your perspective from fear to faith and from panic to purpose.

The Role of Faith in Financial Recovery

Financial failure or loss can be deeply discouraging. I've seen people feel ashamed when they have to start over, close a business, or face debts they didn't anticipate. But faith turns failure into a lesson and recovery into a testimony. It reminds us that our mistakes don't define us; our response does.

I remember a time when my finances hit a low point, and the pressure of unmet responsibilities weighed heavily on me. I didn't have all the answers, but I had the will to rebuild and the faith to try again. I started with what I had, owned my situation, and trusted God to bring people, opportunities, and solutions my way. And in His time, He did it step by step. I do not know how He made a way where there seemed to be no way. I am grateful.

Faith during recovery gives you vision, even when your wallet is empty. It helps you move forward with hope instead of shame. It gives you the courage to try again and the wisdom to do better the second time around.

Faith without financial action is incomplete. But financial plans without divine trust can become burdensome. I've found strength in blending the act of doing my part with trusting God for the outcomes.

Anchors of Trust

In every financial season, whether stable or stormy, I have learned to hold onto a few anchors that keep me grounded:

Prayer and quiet reflection: When I take time to be still, I can hear the wisdom I need. Clarity always follows silence.

Wise counsel: I don't make major financial decisions in isolation. I seek advice from those who've been where I am going. Trusted voices bring calm where confusion wants to reign.

Practical systems: Faith doesn't mean disorganisation. I keep records, create budgets, track expenses, and regularly revisit my plans. These small actions remind me that trust and structure go hand in hand.

Planning and executing family meetings. My husband, our adult children, and I prioritise regular discussions about family finances, adjusting our budgeting, exploring new opportunities, sharing recent financial information on real estate, investment strategies, and other useful ideas in that domain.

Trusting God with finances isn't a passive act. It's a daily practice of surrendering worry, seeking wisdom, and moving forward with faith-filled action. With these anchors, I've found peace even when things didn't look certain and over time, those seeds of trust have produced stability I can stand on.

Trusting God with money isn't just about belief; it's about obedience, surrender, and patience. I've come to understand that no matter how carefully I plan, life can change without warning. Income can shift. Expenses can surprise you. Opportunities can come and go. But in all of that, I've learned to trust that I'm not walking this path alone.

When I surrendered my financial fears to God, I discovered peace. That peace didn't come because all my problems disappeared; it came because I stopped carrying the weight alone. I stopped panicking about the future and started praying with confidence. I began asking, "What is the wise thing to do?" rather than "How do I get quick results?"

I recall seasons when my income was inconsistent, and my responsibilities were numerous. At that time, I prayed more than I spent. I listened more than I complained. And somehow, with God's help, things fell into place. That doesn't mean I didn't work hard; I did, but my trust was not in the hustle. It was in the guidance I received through quiet moments of reflection and divine clarity.

Trusting God with finances also means being a good steward of what's already in your hands. It means not wasting resources just because you believe in more. It means showing responsibility with the little while expecting the increase. That level of trust isn't passive; it's deeply active, practical, and grounded.

Lessons from My Mother's Financial Wisdom

When I think about where my understanding of financial discipline truly began, I think of my mother. I grew up in a home where there wasn't much to spare, especially after my father passed away. But somehow, even in the absence of abundance, my mother always managed to make enough.

She wasn't an accountant, and she didn't have formal financial training. What she had was discipline, clarity, and faith. She planned for every penny, saved what she could, and never allowed today's problems to steal from tomorrow's possibilities. She believed in the strength of small actions, such as saving a little, avoiding waste, and staying focused on what truly mattered: our family's wellness and children's education.

She taught me that dignity doesn't come from how much you have but from how you manage what you have. We never lived under the illusion of luxury, but we lived with stability and intention. That foundation has shaped my perspective on money, and it has guided me through every financial decision I've made since then.

> **Action Step:**
> Write down **three guiding principles** that shape your approach to money. These can be drawn from your faith, upbringing, or personal values. Keep them visible and refer to them whenever you are making a financial decision. Trust the process, take control, and step into a future of financial confidence and freedom.

I often say I became a financial educator long before I was certified. My first classroom was our living room. My first lesson was watching my mother manage scarcity with grace and turn it into sufficiency. Her faith in the face of lack taught me that no situation is hopeless when you lead with wisdom.

Conclusion

You don't need a perfect income, a high-level financial degree, or a flawless past to build a financially stable future; you need wisdom, discipline, and perspective. This chapter has shown that a steady foundation begins with what you believe and how you live that belief daily. Faith in your financial future isn't just about trusting outcomes;

it's about being present, intentional, and grounded in the values that truly matter.

The habits, mindset, and examples you cultivate today are the structures that your financial life will rest on tomorrow. And like any strong foundation, it must be laid deliberately. You have the power to choose this mindset, to align your values with your actions, and to build from wherever you are, whether you have little or a lot to start with. Positive choice brings positive results.

> *Financial stability is not just for a select few; it is possible for you too. With the right mindset, discipline, and action, you can create a life where money serves as a tool, not a burden.*

Your financial future is in your hands. No one else will build it for you. The longer you wait, the longer you stay stuck. Make the decision today to invest in yourself, seek expert guidance, and take control of your future. The future you dream of is possible, but only if you take action now.

We have uncovered the deep connection between belief and behaviour, revealing how faith, whether spiritual, personal, or values-based, can shape and sustain financial decisions. However, even with this foundation, there is another powerful force that often goes unchallenged: the way we think about money itself. Before we build better strategies, we must first uproot the limiting beliefs and mental barriers that quietly control our choices. Let's now explore how our mindset could be the missing key in unlocking lasting financial change.

CHAPTER TWO

MONEY AND MINDSET:

BREAKING FINANCIAL LIMITING BELIEFS

"Do not conform to the pattern of this world, but be transformed by the renewing of your mind."

— Romans 12:2 (NIV)

Money doesn't just live in our wallets; it lives in our minds. Before a person ever earns, saves, or spends, they've already made internal agreements about what they believe is possible. Many of us carry silent, limiting beliefs passed down through generations or shaped by painful experiences, ideas such as "Money is the root of all evil," " rich people are greedy or selfish," "there is never enough money," "making money means I am taking it from someone else," "money is hard to come by," "people like me don't get rich," or "I'm just not good with money."

These beliefs often become invisible barriers, preventing us from achieving financial stability even when the necessary tools and opportunities are within reach. These beliefs hinder open conversations about earning, saving, or investing. That is a misunderstanding of how value and exchange work in an economy.

Some of my close friends think that doing business is dishonest. Understanding and challenging these thoughts is a foundational step toward financial transformation. Because when your thinking shifts, so does your behaviour, and your outcomes soon follow. Continue reading for a deeper understanding of this topic.

Let us affirm that "I don't come from a rich family, therefore a rich family must come from me." Let us have empowering beliefs such as "Money is a tool that can help me do good in the world," "I am capable of learning how to manage and grow my money," "Wealth is available to everyone who seeks it with the right mindset and actions."

When I Thought Money Was Out of My Control

Some of my friends could not manage their money effectively. In fact, for a long time, I believed money controlled them. My early life experiences shaped this mindset, as I grew up in a home where financial struggle was part of everyday reality and where school fees were uncertain. Choices often revolved around survival rather than dreams.

I remember watching my mother stretch every coin with care yet still come up short when school term opened. I witnessed other students being sent back home because their fees hadn't been paid, or they dropped out of school due to a lack of money, and the shame of that experience lingered. It planted in me a quiet fear that no matter how hard families tried, money would always slip through their fingers. They internalised the idea that wealth was for others and that people like us would always have to struggle for every coin.

This belief followed us through school and into adulthood. Even when we began earning money, many people operated with a scarcity mindset, spending impulsively when they had it and fearing the next dry spell. They didn't save because they believed the money wouldn't be enough anyway. They didn't plan because they thought things would fall apart regardless. Our mindset is locked in survival mode.

Shifting My Mindset, Rewriting My Story

However, something began to shift when I started observing people who seemed calm around money, not because they had more, but because they had established systems. They had plans. They didn't panic every time an expense came up. I saw that money management wasn't about how much you had, but how you thought about what you had. That revelation woke something in me.

Slowly, I began to challenge the story my friends had lived by. I told myself that money was a tool, not a master. I initially struggled with budgeting, but I eventually developed a consistent approach. I taught myself to pause before spending and to prioritise saving, even when the amount was small. Each new discipline chipped away at the old belief that money was out of my control.

The Fear of Managing Money

There was a time when I wasn't just worried about having enough; I was afraid of managing it altogether. Budgeting felt intimidating. Saving felt impossible, and investing was unheard of. Most people avoid tracking expenses because they don't want to confront how little they had or how easily it slipped away.

But I've learned that fear keeps you stuck. The more I avoided responsibility, the more powerless I felt. Over time, I realised that facing the fear of writing things down, asking questions, and learning from mistakes wasn't just necessary; it was freeing. Financial peace doesn't come from perfection; it comes from engagement.

From Victim to Steward

It took time, but one of the most empowering shifts in my financial life was realising that I was not a victim of my money; I was its steward. That meant I had the authority to direct, manage, and utilise it in ways that reflected my values and goals.

Becoming a steward shifted everything. I no longer saw money as something that happened to me. I began to see it as something I could influence. Even when I didn't have much, I learned to be intentional. Stewardship gave me back my voice.

Breaking Free from the Scarcity Mindset

Breaking free from a scarcity mindset begins with recognising that it is not just a financial issue; it is a belief system. The scarcity mindset convinces us that there is never enough: not enough money, opportunities, time, or even love. It fosters fear, comparison, and competition, often leading people to cling to what little they have out of anxiety rather than purpose.

This mindset can subtly take root through upbringing, past trauma, or cultural messages that glorify struggle and distrust abundance. Until it's confronted, it quietly shapes choices, relationships, and self-worth, keeping people stuck in survival mode rather than living from a place of vision and faith.

The shift begins internally. Instead of asking, "What if I lose everything?" one must begin asking, "What if there's more than enough?" An abundance mindset isn't about ignoring reality; it's about aligning with truth.

Resources may be limited in any given moment, but creativity, ideas, connections, and divine provision are limitless.

Gratitude is often the first antidote; by acknowledging what already exists, we rewire the brain to expect possibility rather than lack. This shift also demands a renewing of the mind, letting go of limiting beliefs, toxic money stories, or deeply ingrained fears, and replacing them with wisdom, stewardship, and faith in God's ability to provide beyond measure.

Breaking free is not a one-time decision; it's a daily practice. It shows up in how we speak, how we invest in ourselves, how we give, and how we plan for the future. It means refusing to let fear make financial decisions, turning down the volume of self-doubt, and being willing to take risks when purpose demands it. As the scarcity mindset fades, space is created for generosity, collaboration, and vision-led living. True freedom is found not in hoarding what we have but in trusting that what we need will meet us as we step forward in faith and boldness.

Reflection Question:

⌘ What is one financial belief you've carried since childhood, that no longer serves you And what truth would you like to replace it with?

Faith Tested Through Financial Struggles

One of the hardest seasons in my life was struggling to pay my school fees. It was a big burden on my sister and my mother. The pain of being sent home while others stayed in class left more than just academic gaps; it planted emotional wounds and deep-rooted doubts. I didn't feel in control of my future because my education, something so foundational, was constantly threatened by money. It happened few times to fall short on school fees, but I could feel for my friends when it comes to get a clearance from the business office before they can be allowed to take final exams.

Yet, even in the face of disappointment, I kept going. I would walk miles back home with a heavy heart but a determined spirit. As I grew older at the college level, I started doing what I could, helping out in the community, tutoring, typing for others, and taking on any tasks that could earn me a few coins. It wasn't enough to cover all the fees, but it gave me a sense of participation in my future. That struggle refined my perseverance, even when the outcome remained uncertain.

Working Against the Odds

There was no safety net. No one is waiting to bail me out. That meant I had to think creatively about survival and progress. I learned to stretch every franc, to forgo what others saw as essential, and to push myself harder.

Whether it was walking instead of paying for transport, skipping meals to save money, or juggling multiple tasks in one day, I did what had to be done.

I had no means to fix my hair, buy new clothing, or shoes, to the extent that on my graduation day, I had no new suit; I received my diploma wearing a uniform. People may have thought it was humility, but deep inside, I knew that asking my mother for a new dress would be another burden, because she had already done more than enough to pay the school fees for seven years.

At the time, I didn't know these sacrifices were shaping a powerful mindset. Looking back, I realise that those difficult decisions were among the earliest investments in my discipline. They taught me how to delay gratification and focus on long-term gain. That discipline continues to guide me even today.

When Faith Was My Only Resource

In moments when I had nothing left to offer, no income, no plan, and no energy, I turned to the one thing I had: faith. It wasn't just belief in a better future; it was the confidence that my struggle had a purpose. I chose to believe that if I could stay true to what I knew with integrity, honesty, diligence, and resilience, things would eventually shift.

And slowly, they did. Opportunities began to appear, sometimes in subtle ways. Someone would offer me a typing job. I'd have the opportunity to teach someone's child for a small fee. None of it felt big, but together, these moments helped me move forward. Now I strongly believe in multiple streams of income, "one root does not feed a tree."

Faith didn't remove the struggle; it kept my mind and heart from collapsing under it. It gave me something solid to stand on while everything else felt shaky. And now, every time I teach about money or coach someone through their financial pain, I draw from that same place of strength.

Financial struggle taught me more than any classroom could. It taught me to hold on, to stretch beyond what I thought possible, and to keep showing up even when it was hard. I learned to be grateful and satisfied with what I have. Like Paul in Philippians 4:12, I know how to be brought low, and I know how to abound. In any and every circumstance, I have learned the secret of facing plenty and hunger, abundance and need. I know what it's like to be in need, and I know what it's like to have plenty. It was my training ground, and my faith was my fuel.

Wealth, Hard Work, and Self-Reliance on Scripture

Wealth, when gained through honest means and managed with wisdom, is not something to be ashamed of; it's something to be respected and used responsibly. Scripture doesn't shy away from wealth. Instead, it teaches that wealth is a resource that must be stewarded with intention.

Proverbs 10:4 (NIV) says, *"Lazy hands make for poverty, but diligent hands bring wealth."* This verse, among many others, confirms that wealth and hard work are not opposites; they're often companions.

From a young age, I learned to appreciate the value of hard work. It was all around me, modelled especially by my mother, whose discipline was rooted in biblical values even though she never quoted verses. She lived them.

Watching her affirmed in me that wealth is not just about how much you have, but how wisely you manage what you earn. Her example made the idea of self-reliance more than survival; it became a principle of dignity.

Scripture on Self-Reliance and Diligence

Self-reliance isn't about rejecting the community or becoming selfish. It's about doing your part with excellence.

Galatians 6:5 (NIV) says, *"Each one should carry their own load."* That doesn't mean you never need help; it means you take full responsibility for what is in your hands. When we embrace that responsibility, our relationship with money becomes healthier. We stop blaming circumstances and start building from what we have.

The parable of the talents in Matthew 25:14-30 (NIV) also offers a powerful image: those who multiplied what they were given were praised and entrusted with more. But the one who buried his talent out of fear lost it. That story taught me that fear and inaction around money are not harmless; they lead to loss. But diligence and creativity, no matter how small the starting point, lead to growth.

The Balance Between Faith and Work

Some people wait passively for a financial breakthrough, believing faith alone will solve everything. However, the Bible teaches the harmony between belief and effort. James 2:17 (NIV) reminds us that *"faith by itself, if it is not accompanied by action, is dead."* It's not enough to hope things improve; we must rise to the challenge and work with our hands, manage with wisdom, and plan with care.

> **Action Step:**
>
> Write down three limiting beliefs you have about money (e.g., "I will never be rich," "Money is hard to come by," or "I'm not good with finances").
>
> Then, rewrite each belief into a positive and empowering truth (e.g., "I am capable of building wealth through smart decisions" or "I can learn to manage money wisely").
>
> Read these affirmations daily for the next thirty days.

In my life, I experienced transformation not because I sat still and prayed for money to appear, but because I worked while I prayed. I planned while I trusted. I moved while I believed. It was that balance that kept me grounded and moving forward. Wealth became possible not just through belief but through applied faith with direction and purpose.

Conclusion

Your mindset is the gateway to your financial breakthrough. Before strategies or tools, your beliefs either give you permission to grow or bind you to old limitations. What you believe about money, its purpose, accessibility, and your ability to manage it shapes your actions long before any income arrives.

Breaking free from limiting beliefs requires intentional unlearning and courageous relearning. It's not always easy, but it is always possible. And when your mind is renewed, your money can finally follow.

> *The way you think about money shapes your financial reality. Choose to believe that wealth, security, and financial success are within your reach because they are.*

Understanding how mindset influences money is only one piece of the puzzle. Without financial education, even the best mindset can leave you directionless. That's why the next step is to gain knowledge by learning what schools never taught and what experience has proven essential. Financial literacy is the cornerstone of stability, and ignoring it comes at a significant cost that we have yet to understand fully.

CHAPTER THREE

THE PRICE OF FINANCIAL IGNORANCE

"My people are destroyed for lack of knowledge."

— Hosea 4:6 (NIV)

Before you can master money, you must first understand it. Yet, for many, financial education is the missing piece, the one tool they were never given but desperately need. In many homes, money is either a taboo topic or one wrapped in silence, secrecy, or shame. Schools rarely teach how to budget, save, invest, or prepare for the future. As a result, too many adults are left to figure things out through trial and error, usually at a high cost.

Financial ignorance isn't just an innocent gap in knowledge; it's a trap. It leads to debt, missed opportunities, poor choices, and constant anxiety. It locks people in cycles of survival because they don't know there's a better way. But ignorance can be replaced. With awareness, learning, and a commitment to growth, anyone can transition from confusion to confidence and from living paycheck to paycheck to building a lasting future.

In this chapter, we reconnoitre why financial education is non-negotiable and how knowledge, when applied, becomes your most powerful asset on the path to stability.

Understanding the Impact of Childhood Experiences

Growing up in a home where financial challenges were frequent, I absorbed certain philosophies without realising it. I saw money as something unpredictable, there one day and gone the next. My mother did her best to make ends meet, and while her resilience inspired me, our constant financial instability taught me to expect lack rather than abundance.

We didn't talk openly about money, not because it wasn't important, but because it always felt heavy, like something to worry about, not to understand. This silence shaped my mindset. I came to believe that money was a struggle, not a skill, a burden, not a tool. These childhood impressions clung to me long into adulthood.

As I started earning money, I noticed patterns that I didn't know how to explain. I'd spend quickly, rarely plan, and often feel anxious, even when I had enough. It wasn't until I began learning about financial literacy that I realised how much of my behaviour was rooted in my upbringing. The emotional weight of scarcity, shame, and secrecy continued to influence my financial decisions.

Acknowledging the impact of my early experiences allowed me to break free from their hold. I began to unlearn what I'd unknowingly carried and made space to build new beliefs; ones rooted in wisdom, discipline, and hope. Our childhood experiences leave deep marks, but they don't have to determine our financial future. With reflection and education, we can rewrite the script and choose a more empowered path forward.

The Messages I Absorbed Without Words

I never heard phrases like "investing," "budgeting," or "emergency fund" while growing up, (mama said don't spend all the money, keep some for dispensary) she meant "emergency fund" but I heard enough silence and saw enough struggle to shape how I thought money worked. I learned that it was stressful. That created tension. That it could disappear without warning, without being explicitly told, I came to believe that money was something we endured, not something we managed.

The way adults around me handled financial hardship taught me that money problems were shameful and best kept quiet. I didn't realise that this secrecy would later shape how I avoided difficult conversations or failed to plan. These silent messages were powerful, and they lingered into my adult life until I learned to recognise and challenge them.

Repeating Patterns I Didn't Understand

When I started making money, I fell into habits that I thought were just part of my personality: spending my money immediately, feeling anxious at the idea of long-term plans, and constantly bracing for financial setbacks. It took time and intentional learning to realise these weren't just random behaviours. They were patterns born from emotional wounds that hadn't healed.

Once I started identifying the patterns of scarcity, fear, and emotional spending, I could begin to change them. I realised I wasn't broken; I was acting out of unresolved conditioning. That awareness gave me power. I started budgeting, saving little by little, and saying no to the pressure of keeping up appearances. I permitted myself to grow beyond the cycle I had inherited.

Rewriting the Money Script

Healing is choosing what happens next. I decided to rewrite the narrative I had lived with for so long. I started speaking openly about money, asking questions, seeking help, and eventually teaching others.

Instead of avoiding financial topics, I now embrace them. Instead of assuming money will disappear, I plan for it to grow. And instead of feeling shame about my past, I use it as a foundation for wisdom. The process is still ongoing, but every step I take reshapes the story, and I know now that I'm the one holding the pen.

Healing Deep-rooted Emotional Wounds

Apart from being numbers, money is tied to our emotions, our past, and our sense of worth. For many of us, emotional wounds tied to finances run deep. They were formed in childhood, reinforced by experiences of lack, shame, or silence, and buried under years of struggling to survive instead of thriving. I know this because I've experienced it firsthand. I didn't just need to learn how to manage money; I needed to heal from what money had come to represent: anxiety, fear, and self-doubt.

I remember how painful it was to walk away from conversations about money. When I couldn't contribute or when I was struggling, I kept quiet. I believed that financial difficulty was a reflection of personal failure. So, I smiled, dressed up, and tried to maintain appearances even when I was sinking beneath the surface. These emotional patterns, avoidance, guilt, and secrecy kept me trapped. It wasn't until I faced them that things began to change.

Healing started with honesty. I had to admit where it hurt, name the lies I had believed, and forgive myself for what I didn't know. Financial education provided me with tools, but emotional healing gave me the courage to utilise them. I began to separate my value from my bank balance. I stopped comparing myself to others. I started telling the truth to myself and eventually to others about where I was and where I wanted to be.

I also learned to forgive my past, the people who didn't know better, and the systems that had failed to prepare me. This forgiveness softened my heart and sharpened my focus. I no longer made decisions from a place of fear but from a place of clarity and calm. That inner shift made my outer strategies sustainable.

To anyone reading this who feels that their money problems are more emotional than mathematical, you're not alone. Healing is part of your financial breakthrough. You must repair the emotional foundation so that when the tools arrive, you can utilise them effectively. Shame has no place in your future. Courage does.

And with each step you take, learning, growing, and forgiving, you begin to see money not as a source of pain but as a resource for peace, purpose, and freedom.

Reflection Question:

- ⌘ What unspoken emotional wounds or financial fears have shaped your relationship with money and what would healing from them make possible for you?

From Self-doubt to Self-acceptance

There was a time I didn't believe I was the kind of person who could succeed financially. I thought financial success belonged to other people who came from wealthy families, those who spoke confidently about money, or those with high-paying jobs.

I didn't see myself in that picture. Academically brilliant, I was the girl who struggled to stay in school, who was sent home due to unpaid fees, and who worked odd jobs to survive. My confidence had been chipped away by real-life experiences that made me feel small.

That self-doubt didn't just affect my emotions; it shaped my choices. I played it safe with opportunities. I undercharged for my services. I stayed silent in rooms where I could have spoken up. Even when I had a gift or an idea, I second-guessed it. I was hardworking, but I lacked self-belief. And for a long time, I didn't realise that this internal hesitation was costing me more than just money; it was costing me progress.

Nonetheless, self-acceptance began to grow quietly, first as a whisper that maybe, just maybe, I had something to offer. When people around me started to affirm what they saw in me, I leaned in, slowly. When I learned how to manage even the little I had, it built my confidence. When I could teach someone else how to budget or save, I realised my knowledge had value. It wasn't dramatic or overnight, but it was real.

Self-acceptance doesn't mean pretending to have it all together. It means acknowledging your worth even as you grow. It's the decision to say, "I may not be where I want to be yet, but I belong in this space. I deserve stability. I am capable of learning, earning, and leading." That inner affirmation became a quiet strength that pushed me to pursue certification as a financial professional, to speak publicly, and to serve clients with confidence.

Financial growth requires more than skill; it requires belief. When I started believing in myself, opportunities began to appear in a different light. I applied for more. I reached out. I charged better. And I stopped shrinking in spaces where I was meant to contribute. That's the gift of self-acceptance: it makes room for you to grow without apology.

Reclaiming Personal Power Embedded in Truth

There comes a moment when pretending no longer serves you. When the desire to grow becomes stronger than the fear of being seen, that's when truth becomes a turning point, not just about what's happening in your life, but about what you believe and what you are willing to reclaim. For me, reclaiming personal power began when I stopped running from my financial reality and chose to face it with honesty and integrity.

The truth was I had made mistakes. I had lived small because I believed I had no other option. I had avoided responsibility in some areas because I felt unequipped. However, the truth didn't come to shame me. It came to free me. I started telling the truth about what I didn't know, what I was afraid of, and where I needed help. And as uncomfortable as it was, that truth gave me my voice back.

When you reclaim power, you stop waiting for permission. You stop blaming others. You stop defining yourself by your past. You begin to see that your current reality doesn't have to be your final one. I learned to own my story, not just the strength but also the struggle. And that honesty gave me clarity. It gave me the ability to set goals that mattered, to seek knowledge I once avoided, and to step into roles I had never imagined myself worthy of.

I reclaimed power by aligning with the truth, my truth. Not someone else's expectations or definitions of success. I stopped striving to meet standards that didn't reflect my values. Instead, I focused on building a life that honoured what mattered most to me: security, wisdom, purpose, and peace.

Real power doesn't come from external status. It's found in the quiet decision to live authentically, to grow intentionally, and to keep moving forward no matter where you start. That kind of power can't be taken; it can only be reclaimed. And once you reclaim it, your financial transformation is no longer a wish. It becomes a reality you're actively creating.

> **Action Step:**
>
> **Write a letter to yourself** from the perspective of truth. In that letter, affirm your ability to grow, acknowledge where you've been holding back, and speak to the financial life you believe you deserve.
>
> **Let this be your written declaration** of power reclaimed, not based on perfection, but on your willingness to live from the truth, starting now.

Conclusion

Emotional wounds, unresolved self-doubt, and misaligned beliefs can quietly undermine your financial progress, regardless of how much you earn or how skilled you become. But the good news is that healing is possible, and power can be reclaimed.

When you begin to do the inner work of acknowledging past pain, speaking the truth about your experiences, and choosing acceptance over shame, you create space for lasting financial growth. This chapter has shown that real change doesn't begin in your wallet; it begins in your heart and your mind. The financial strategies may come later, but this inner reset is what ensures they work.

> *What you don't know about money can cost you more than you realise. The more knowledge you gain, the more control you have over your future. Continue reading this book, your financial success depends on it.*

Now that you've addressed the internal limitations and reclaimed your sense of worth, it's time to build habits that reflect that healing. Financial freedom requires more than knowledge; it also demands discipline. How can delayed gratification and intentional choices become the backbone of a truly stable financial life from the perspective of truth?

CHAPTER FOUR

FINANCIAL DISCIPLINE AND DELAYED GRATIFICATION

"The plans of the diligent lead to profit as surely as haste leads to poverty."

—Proverbs 21:5 (NIV)

Financial discipline is choosing what matters most. It's the consistent ability to manage money with foresight, control, and intention, even when immediate desires try to steer you off track. In a world of quick fixes and instant gratification, discipline teaches us the value of patience and waiting. It is the bridge between our goals and our habits, between financial freedom and financial frustration.

Many people don't struggle with income; they struggle with impulse. And the difference between temporary wealth and lasting stability often lies in our ability to delay gratification. Whether it's resisting a spontaneous purchase or sticking to a long-term savings goal, discipline is a muscle that must be trained daily.

Let us discover what it means to exercise self-control, distinguish between needs and wants, learn to wait, and remain committed to long-term rewards even when short-term sacrifices are necessary.

The Power of Self-control in Finances

Financial self-control is one of the most underrated yet essential tools for building a stable and fulfilling life. It's not always about how much you earn but how well you manage what you have. I learned early on that earning money doesn't automatically bring peace. Without self-control, money slips through your hands no matter how much you make.

We see people who had money in their pocket, but because they hadn't trained themselves to pause before spending, they ended up making decisions that left them regretful and broke. Whether it was buying items they didn't need or trying to keep up with others socially, they were often reacting rather than making a conscious choice. That reactive living became expensive not just financially but emotionally.

When I started practising self-control, everything changed. I began to pause and ask myself: Do I need this, or do I want it now? Can this wait? What will this decision ultimately cost me? I realised that every financial choice had a ripple effect. By saying no in the short term, I was saying yes to something bigger, like peace of mind, future opportunities, or reaching my goals without anxiety.

Self-control doesn't mean you never enjoy your money. It means you spend with purpose. You stop giving power to emotional spending and start placing value on your future. This mindset helped me stop the cycle of constantly starting over. Instead of always recovering from poor decisions, I began building on good ones. And the more I practised, the stronger that discipline became. Financial self-control is not just a tool; it's a way of life.

Biblical Wisdom on Self-control and Money

The Bible consistently highlights self-control as a defining characteristic of the wise and faithful. Proverbs 25:28 (NIV) says, *"Like a city whose walls are broken through is a person who lacks self-control."* This verse paints a picture of vulnerability, how a lack of discipline exposes us to unnecessary harm, including financial ruin. When we live without boundaries or restraint, we become more susceptible to poor choices that weaken our stability.

In the New Testament, Galatians 5:22-23 (NIV) lists self-control as one of the fruits of the Spirit. It is not just a personal trait but a spiritual strength that grows through intentional practice. When we apply this principle to finances, it means that our spending, saving, and giving should be guided by thoughtfulness rather than impulse.

1 Corinthians 9:25 (NIV) also says, *"Everyone who competes in the games goes into strict training. They do it to get a crown that will not last."* Likewise, financial discipline is a form of training that chooses future gain over instant reward.

These scriptures remind us that managing money with self-control is not only practical but deeply spiritual. It honours God, respects our resources, and positions us to live with purpose rather than pressure.

Needs vs. Wants

One of the most liberating lessons I've ever learned was understanding the distinction between a need and a want. It seems simple, but in a world that markets desire as a necessity, the lines often blur. Needs are essential to survival and progress: food, shelter, education, and healthcare. Wants, on the other hand, are things we desire, often emotionally, to feel good, fit in, or experience pleasure in the moment.

Growing up, I didn't always have the luxury of choosing between needs and wants. Everything felt urgent. Merely, I observed that when my friends finally had money of their own, they found it easy to justify spending on things they had gone without for years. That is how I soon learned that giving in to every want, even if it seemed small, created a pattern of scarcity. The essentials would go unmet while short-lived pleasures were satisfied for many families. My mother lived on sacrificing for others; thus, I followed in her footsteps.

I had to start asking myself deeper questions: Will this purchase improve my life beyond today? Am I trying to impress someone or reward myself for a tough season? Could this money serve me better somewhere else? That reflection helped me redefine my priorities.

True financial maturity is seen in how well you can delay what you want for what you need most. It's about being able to say no now so you can say yes later, with peace of mind, stability, or even greater opportunities. Budgeting became easier when I separated the two. It no longer felt like a sacrifice. It felt like wisdom.

When you understand the distinction between needs and wants, you stop chasing fleeting satisfaction and begin investing in your long-term well-being. That's not just financial discipline; it's emotional intelligence in action.

Reflection Question:

⌘ What is one "want" that often gets in the way of your financial progress, and what need or goal could you prioritise instead if you choose to wait?

The Value of Waiting

"But they that wait upon the Lord, shall renew their strength,"

—Isaiah 40:31

In a world that celebrates speed, waiting has become one of the rarest virtues. However, when it comes to money, waiting can be one of the wisest decisions you make. The ability to delay gratification is about willpower, clarity, maturity, and trust in the bigger picture. I've learned that waiting doesn't mean doing nothing; it means preparing, planning, and positioning yourself for better outcomes.

There were many seasons when I had to say no, not because I didn't want something, but because I had a greater goal in mind. Saying no to temporary pleasures helped me say yes to long-term peace. I remember resisting the urge to move into a more expensive home, even when I could afford the rent, because I had a bigger vision for my children's education and my business capital. That choice wasn't easy, but it brought lasting rewards.

Waiting also builds character. It teaches you that trends, emotions, or peer pressure do not dictate your actions. You begin to define your life by principles, not pressure. Each time you delay gratification and stay focused on your priorities, you're strengthening your financial muscles.

Some of the best financial decisions I've made didn't feel exciting at the time. They felt slow, quiet, even boring. But in hindsight, they were exactly what I needed. The money I didn't spend, the commitments I postponed, and the luxuries I put on hold allowed me to invest in what truly mattered. And that kind of financial discipline doesn't just build wealth; it builds wisdom.

Why Waiting Aligns with Faithful Living

At the heart of this book is the conviction that building lasting financial stability requires more than quick wins and emotional spending. It calls for smart choices grounded in self-awareness, trust, and intentional growth. Waiting reinforces this by teaching us how to honour our goals above our impulses. Every time we choose patience over pressure, we are declaring our commitment to a lifestyle that values purpose over performance.

Waiting is where faith meets wisdom; it's a space where we allow time to do its work while we stay faithful to our vision. This principle is embedded throughout the book: choosing to learn before earning, building before displaying, and preparing before expanding. Whether you are saving for a dream, building your family's future, or avoiding debt, the discipline of waiting protects what you're building.

The Long-Term Reward of Financial Discipline

One of the most underestimated benefits of financial discipline is its compounding effect over time. Every wise decision you make today, no matter how small, adds up to a life of stability, freedom, and peace. The reward doesn't come overnight, but it always comes. Whether it's finally being able to afford an investment, retire with dignity, or give generously to others, disciplined choices open doors that shortcuts never will.

I've seen firsthand how consistent savings, even in small amounts, have provided my family and me with relief during difficult seasons. I've experienced firsthand how budgeting helped me escape the chaos of living paycheck to paycheck and establish a rhythm of financial confidence. The sacrifices I made in the early years were difficult, but they ultimately protected my future.

The truth is that financial discipline is a form of love. It's how we honour our goals, respect our responsibilities, and create peace for ourselves and those who depend on us. It's about taking control without being controlled. When discipline becomes a lifestyle, the long-term rewards are not just financial gain but also clarity, dignity, and purpose.

And best of all? It's never too late to start. Whether you're just learning or starting over, the rewards of discipline are always waiting to meet your commitment.

> **Action Step:**
>
> For the next 30 days, track every single purchase you make. Review your spending at the end of the month and identify areas where you could have exercised more discipline. Challenge yourself to delay one unnecessary purchase and redirect that money toward savings or debt repayment.

Conclusion

Financial discipline is a foundational pillar in building a life of peace and progress. It's not about saying "no" to everything you want; it's about learning to say "yes" to the things that truly matter. When you choose self-control, distinguish between needs and wants, embrace the beauty of waiting, and remain committed to long-term goals, you're not just managing money; you're cultivating a more fulfilling life. You're mastering your future.

> *Every dollar you manage wisely today is a step toward the financial freedom you desire tomorrow. Stay patient, stay focused, and trust that the sacrifices you make now will create a future of stability and success.*

This chapter wasn't written to glorify sacrifice but to highlight the power of intentional living. Your ability to delay gratification is a testament to your growth, vision, and courage. If you've made it this far, you've already proven that discipline isn't beyond you but rather within you. With continued commitment, financial freedom becomes more than just a dream. It becomes a pattern.

Lessons From Part One: Foundations of Faith and Finance

* Ground your financial decisions in something bigger than fear or survival. Whether through faith or values, having an anchor helps you stay focused during uncertain times.

* Reflect on the money messages you absorbed growing up. Understanding your past helps you break free from repeating unhealthy patterns.

* Don't ignore what you don't know. Invest time in learning about money, including budgeting, saving, insurance, and investing. The cost of ignorance is too high.

* Make space for emotional healing. Shame, self-doubt, and financial trauma must be addressed if you're going to move forward with confidence.

* Practice daily discipline by saying no to everything and consistently choosing what aligns with your future.

* Ask yourself, "Is this a need or a want?" That simple question can protect your wallet and your peace of mind.'

* Be okay with waiting, as delayed gratification doesn't mean denial. It means direction. Let patience protect your progress.

* Let discipline become a rhythm, not a punishment. The reward is clarity, control, and peace, which money can't buy.

With these lessons in place, we are now moving on to Part Two: *Smart Strategies for Money Management*. This is where faith-inspired vision meets practical tools.

If the first part redefined your internal landscape, what follows will strengthen your financial systems. It's time to act on what you believe, structure what you've imagined, and begin building the future you've already made room for.

PART II

SMART STRATEGIES FOR MONEY MANAGEMENT

CHAPTER FIVE

BUDGETING WITH PURPOSE

"Whoever gathers money little by little makes it grow."

— Proverbs 13:11b (NIV)

Budgeting is the intentional act of guiding your resources toward what matters most. Through careful planning and disciplined tracking, you transform uncertainty into clarity. I once believed that budgeting meant sacrificing every small pleasure and living under constant restriction. Over time, I discovered that budgeting becomes a liberating practice rather than a confinement when I direct each dollar toward a purpose rooted in stewardship.

My financial life shifted when I viewed money decisions through the lens of my values: honouring God, providing for my family, and preparing for the seasons ahead. In this chapter, I share how I recognised patterns of survival-mode spending, learned to plan intentionally, and found resilience and freedom by giving every dollar a role.

These insights blend experiences from my life, including tracking allowances as a student and adjusting habits across relocations in different countries with varying economies, with practical principles supported by research. Like Apostle Paul, I learn how to live in abundance and scarcity.

Recognising the Signs of Living in Survival Mode

I remember, like many people, ending many months wondering, "Where did all the money go?" As a student living on a tight allowance, rent would absorb most of what we received, and we scrambled to cover essentials.

I began writing down every expense in a journal: "Today I spent this," "Today I paid that."

Documenting outlays revealed patterns I had previously ignored: small, unplanned purchases, occasional dining out, and unneeded items that had accumulated. Seeing entries on paper exposed habits of living, reacting to paying bills at the last minute, relying on credit for routine needs, and feeling anxiety whenever an unexpected cost arose

Signs include:

- ⌘ Surprise bills that derail other plans.
- ⌘ Repeated borrowing or reliance on credit to fill gaps.

- ⌘ Neglect of savings because every shilling seems spoken for.
- ⌘ Anxiety whenever income arrives, instead of relief.

These patterns create a cycle: working harder does not yield calm, only more exhaustion. Recognising survival mode is the first step. I recall nights worrying about school fees for my children or unexpected medical costs for elderly relatives. Admitting the need for a plan freed me from shame and opened the door to change.

In Rwanda, my mother taught me that clear priorities brought peace despite scarce resources. The money she had was under the tablecloth in front of her bed, for us to use every day, along with some other amount in her purse, and a bank account in a distant location where we could travel for half a day to conduct transactions.

During times of instability, when enemies were stealing and destroying homes, she would place money outside under a secure stone, trusting that preparation could protect against uncertainty. These practices reveal the remedy for survival mode: awareness of precariousness and simple, consistent preparation.

Awareness of Survival-Mode Indicators

Financial stress often manifests physically and mentally. Financial worries can contribute to anxiety, depression, headaches, insomnia, and even cardiovascular strain.

Research shows that persistent financial concerns correlate with elevated psychological distress and physiological symptoms such as tension headaches or sleep disturbances. Recognising these signals in oneself or others is a vital first step toward addressing underlying patterns rather than dismissing them as personal failure.

Many individuals live paycheck to paycheck, deciding which bills to cover now and which to defer until the next cycle. Behavioural economics studies describe how resource scarcity increases cognitive load, leading to a narrowed focus on immediate shortfalls at the expense of longer-term priorities. Understanding that this experience is widespread can help normalise the challenge and motivate proactive shifts rather than isolation or shame.

Under financial pressure, decision-making often defaults to fight, flight, or freeze responses. For example, impulsive small purchases may serve as temporary relief from stress, avoiding balance checks may feel like escaping discomfort, and postponing bill payments may seem easier than facing anxiety directly. Research indicates that stress-induced impulses can drive such behaviours, impair cognitive control and lead to patterns that reinforce survival-mode spending. Recognising these tendencies in oneself allows intentional interruption of reactive habits.

The scarcity mindset narrows attention to urgent needs, often sidelining broader objectives such as saving or giving. Behavioural research demonstrates that when resources feel insufficient, mental bandwidth is consumed by immediate concerns, reducing capacity for planning and self-regulation. Identifying when this tunnel vision arises enables a conscious shift: creating small "slack" buffers or mental reminders of long-term goals to counter the narrowing effect.

Reflecting on faith traditions, the example of Joseph's preparation for a season of famine, such as storing food during years of plenty, illustrates proactive planning rather than panic. Empirical studies also show that religious involvement and positive spiritual coping can buffer the effects of financial hardship on mental health, reducing distress and promoting resilience. Recognising whether anxiety arises from a lack of planning or deeper distrust can guide both practical steps and faith-based encouragement.

Expense tracking offers a concrete way to move from vague worry to actionable clarity. Research into self-regulatory financial behaviours finds that persistent expense tracking correlates with reduced discretionary spending and heightened awareness of spending patterns.

However, it may not guarantee perfect adherence to budgets. Using apps or manual journals can reveal spending "leaks" and inform targeted adjustments. Tracking serves awareness, not self-condemnation; the goal is to identify trends and redirect resources toward priorities.

Discussing financial stress with trusted individuals can provide support and accountability. Studies indicate that sharing concerns, whether in faith communities, peer groups, or with mentors, can alleviate feelings of isolation and reinforce commitment to change. Collaborating on solutions or simply verbalising worries often reduces cognitive burden and opens pathways for collective problem-solving, making recognition of survival-mode patterns a shared, constructive process.

Shifting from Reactivity to Intentional Living

I began by setting priorities before spending, categorising them into six areas: housing, utilities, necessities, essentials, savings, and discretionary items. When I had only a small remainder after rent and core costs, I still "paid myself first" by moving a portion into savings immediately upon receipt, even if modest. I learned to adjust my habits by eating at home instead of dining out and choosing simpler celebrations, so that each choice aligned with my longer-term goals.

Prayerfully, I asked for wisdom to discern what mattered and committed to a zero-based approach where every dollar was assigned a role. Each month, I reviewed actual spending against the plan, and when life shifted, I revised allocations to account for new expenses or income changes before problems emerged. Trusting God while acting responsibly became a pattern: I planned rather than waiting for crises to force adjustments.

Practical strategies include:

- ⌘ Zero-based budgeting: assign every dollar a role (expenses, savings, giving).
- ⌘ Envelope or bucket method: physically or digitally allocate funds to categories to avoid overspending.
- ⌘ Regular budget review: monthly check-ins to compare actual spending vs. plan, adjusting categories as life changes.
- ⌘ Aligning budget categories with values: e.g., designating a portion for generosity, ministry, or charitable giving as integral, not an afterthought.
- ⌘ Buffer funds: Building a small buffer prevents derailment when unexpected expenses arise.

In faith tradition, intentional budgeting can be prayerfully guided: seeking wisdom (James 1:5) in discerning priorities, entrusting outcomes to God while acting responsibly. I habitually documented every expense ("I write down what I spent today; trace where my money goes…"), because I found it foundational to understanding my spending habits and enabling me to reallocate my money intentionally.

Reflection Questions:

- ⌘ Am I telling my money where to go, or am I constantly wondering where it went?
- ⌘ How well does my current spending align with my financial goals?

Practical Steps to Build Resilience

Resilience in financial management refers to an individual, household, or organisation's capacity to withstand, cope with, and recover from adverse financial events or shocks. At its core, this concept encompasses more than simply having resources; it involves dynamic processes and behaviours that enable one to respond effectively when unexpected expenses, income disruptions, or broader economic downturns occur.

Studies describe financial resilience as the ability to access emergency funds from various sources when needed and rely on internal resources (such as savings, skills, and mindset) and external supports (such as social networks, insurance, and community programs) to navigate hardship.

Key components of financial resilience include building and maintaining an emergency fund, diversifying income streams, managing debt responsibly, and continuously enhancing financial literacy. An emergency fund provides a cushion against temporary income reductions or sudden expenses, thereby reducing the need for high-cost borrowing.

Diversified income, such as side activities, investments, or multiple revenue streams, reduces vulnerability if one income source fails. Responsible debt management prevents obligations from overwhelming cash flow, while ongoing learning about budgeting, saving, and risk management equips individuals to make informed decisions under stress.

Behavioural and psychological factors also play a significant role. Financial self-efficacy, the belief in one's ability to manage money, correlates with proactive budgeting and saving behaviours, reinforcing resilience when challenges arise. Mindsets oriented toward planning, adaptability, and reframing setbacks as learning opportunities support steady progress despite disruptions.

Regular "health checks" of finances, scenario planning for plausible shocks, and leveraging social capital (discussing plans with trusted peers or advisors) help maintain preparedness and reduce anxiety-driven decisions.

From a broader perspective, resilience in financial management aligns with risk management but extends beyond it. Rather than only identifying and mitigating potential threats, resilience involves preparing adaptive responses and recovery strategies when shocks occur. This includes establishing contingency plans (e.g., "if income falls by X, then I will reduce discretionary spending by Y and draw on emergency savings"), securing access to supportive resources (insurance, community assistance), and maintaining flexibility to adjust long-term goals as circumstances change.

Building resilience means preparing for variability in income or expenses. A family should maintain budgeting discipline through multiple moves and varying income streams. Key practices:

- ⌘ Emergency fund planning: Start small, build to cover at least one month's expenses, then three to six months. Even as students, setting aside a nominal amount each period builds resilience over time.

- ⌘ Scenario planning: Imagine "what if income drops?" and pre-decide adjustments rather than scrambling under stress.

- ⌘ Multiple income mindset: Although the primary focus here is budgeting, resilience is enhanced when budgeting is paired with exploring additional income avenues (foreshadows Part Three).

- ⌘ Community support: Budget conversations with spouses and families foster shared understanding; as I noted, family teamwork in budgeting prevents conflicts and reinforces collective goals.

- ⌘ Seasonal adjustments: Budgeting must adapt to life stages (e.g., pregnancy, schooling, relocation). Regularly revisiting categories ensures relevance.

How to Thrive in Daily Life

Beyond survival, purposeful budgeting frees resources for thriving, investing in growth, generosity, and rest. From transcript: choosing affordable alternatives (cooking at home, simpler celebrations) freed funds for savings or charitable giving, yielding financial and spiritual dividends.

Thriving also involves:

- ⌘ Allocating for growth: budgeting for learning (books, courses) as an investment in future earning potential.

- ⌘ Prioritising health: Ensuring the budget includes healthy food and preventive care, avoiding greater costs later.

- ⌘ Joy within limits: Setting aside a modest "fun" fund ensures that disciplined budgeting isn't joyless; this fosters sustainability.

- ⌘ Generosity as budgeted: Regular giving aligns finances with faith, reinforces trust, and cultivates gratitude.

> **Action Step:**
> Create a **monthly budget** that includes **your income, fixed expenses, savings, and discretionary spending**. Track your expenses for the next 30 days and adjust where necessary to ensure your spending aligns with your financial goals.

Conclusion

Budgeting with purpose transforms finances from a source of anxiety into a framework for faithful stewardship. You build resilience and freedom by documenting expenses, setting intentional priorities, and aligning spending with values.

> *A budget is not a restriction; it's a strategy for financial freedom. Every dollar you plan wisely today is a step toward financial stability and peace of mind.*

The lesson: budgeting is not merely a restriction, but an empowerment; each dollar directed thoughtfully becomes a tool for stability, generosity, and growth. As you cultivate this discipline, you'll find that purposeful planning demonstrates absolute trust in God's provision and unlocks possibilities for impact that extend beyond yourself.

CHAPTER SIX

THE DISCIPLINE OF SAVING

"Go to the ant, you sluggard; consider its ways and be wise."

— Proverbs 6:6 (NIV)

Saving often competes with immediate needs or desires, yet saving is an act of wisdom and preparation in faithful stewardship. It reflects trust in God while exercising discipline. Building on the budgeting foundation, this chapter digs deeper into cultivating saving habits, establishing emergency funds, and thinking beyond today toward future needs and opportunities.

The Habit of Saving

Saving consistently requires a mindset shift: viewing saving not as optional but as essential. From the transcript: even when income was limited (e.g., a student budget with rent high relative to income), I prioritised the principle of "pay yourself first," setting aside a portion before other spending.

Cultivating such a habit involves:

Automating savings involves setting up a system where a fixed portion of each income deposit moves directly into a separate account before you see the remaining balance.

I set up an automatic transfer on payday so that saving happens without conscious effort; this means I never face the temptation to spend the money first. When the transfer occurs immediately, I treat that amount as already allocated, and my spending decisions adjust to the leftover funds.

Over time, this approach removed the need for willpower each month and consistently built a habit of saving. If circumstances change, such as fluctuations in income, I revisit the percentage but maintain the practice of directing funds to savings first, ensuring the discipline remains intact.

Starting small creates momentum. I began by saving as little as five percent of my income, understanding that even modest amounts accumulate meaningfully over time. When I saw the balance grow, I felt encouraged to increase the allocation to seven or ten percent, and later to a slightly higher amount as my income increased.

This gradual scaling prevented overwhelm and maintained positive reinforcement: each milestone felt achievable rather than daunting. I built confidence in the habit by starting with an amount that didn't strain my budget. Over months and years, incremental increases compounded, transforming a small initial effort into a substantial cushion without creating undue financial stress.

Mental framing shifts saving from an optional leftover to a must-pay obligation. I treated the savings transfer like a fixed bill, which was non-negotiable and part of my core expenses. When planning my budget, I listed savings alongside rent, utilities, and essentials, ensuring they held equal importance.

This mindset prevented me from skipping or delaying deposits when other desires arose. Viewing saving as mandatory reinforced consistency and anchored my financial decisions: discretionary spending was only considered what remained after saving, never before. This change in perspective cemented saving as a priority rather than a reward for leftover funds.

Visual tracking reinforces the saving habit by making progress tangible and visible. I created basic charts showing month-by-month balances and occasionally reviewed growth trends to see how early small deposits led to larger totals.

Watching the line or bar rise provided motivation to maintain or increase contributions. When I reached a milestone, such as my first emergency fund target, I marked it visibly, celebrating the achievement before setting the next goal. Visual cues can include a graph in a budgeting app, a handwritten chart on paper, or a spreadsheet highlighting progress. Regularly observing these visuals kept me engaged and reminded me that consistent action yields concrete results, which in turn sustains the habit.

Behavioural research shows that automation and pre-commitment inadvertently reduce the temptation to spend saved funds. In a faith context, saving acknowledges stewardship of what God entrusts, preparing for seasons of scarcity or opportunities to bless others.

Paying Yourself First

The principle of paying yourself first means allocating a portion of each income receipt into savings or investment before addressing other expenses. This approach shifts saving from an afterthought to a priority, ensuring that resources for future needs or goals accumulate automatically.

Treating saving as a mandatory allocation, individuals avoid the common pattern of spending first and hoping something remains for savings. Instead, the planned transfer occurs immediately when income arrives, and the remaining balance guides spending decisions.

Adopting this principle builds financial discipline. When savings happen automatically, there is no need to rely on willpower each month. Over time, consistent deposits into a separate account create a growing buffer for emergencies, planned goals, or longer-term objectives.

Observing that a steady habit reinforces confidence in one's ability to manage money effectively. This confidence often extends into other behaviours, such as more mindful spending and proactive planning for future expenses.

Implementation typically begins by choosing a realistic percentage of income to save. Starting with a modest proportion, such as five or ten percent, allows the habit to form without straining the regular budget.

As comfort and income grow, the percentage can increase. Automated transfers on payday or regular deposit dates ensure the allocation happens before discretionary choices. Keeping savings in a distinct account reinforces separation from spending funds and reduces the temptation to dip into the cushion for non-emergencies.

Aligning the saved amount with clear goals enhances motivation. Naming savings buckets, such as an emergency fund, education fund, or a future project, connects each deposit to a specific purpose. Periodic reviews help adjust targets when circumstances change, such as shifts in income or evolving priorities.

When unexpected costs arise, the existing balance provides peace of mind. After using any portion of the savings, promptly rebuilding the allocation maintains the habit. Over time, paying yourself first establishes a reliable foundation that underpins resilience, supports planned ambitions, and encourages generosity when opportunities to give or invest appear.

Here's some practical guidance:

Determine a Realistic Percentage. I began by examining my income and regular expenses to identify what felt sustainable for saving. I listed fixed commitments, rent, utilities, essential bills, and variable costs, such as groceries and transportation.

From there, I tested different percentages for directing into savings, starting with a modest amount that would not strain day-to-day needs. For example, I might initially set aside five percent of my earnings, ensuring that I can meet my obligations without pressure.

Over time, as I became comfortable with this habit and as income occasionally rose, I gradually increased the percentage. This steady scaling reinforced confidence: seeing that I could live well on what remained encouraged me to raise the allocation. Your assessment follows the same principle: review your cash flow honestly, choose an amount you can commit to consistently, and plan to adjust upward when circumstances allow. This way, saving becomes a reliable practice rather than an occasional afterthought.

Separate Accounts. I opened a dedicated savings account separate from my spending account, so the reserved funds felt set apart and less tempting to use for daily expenses. Whenever income arrived, the automated transfer landed in this account, and I no longer debated whether to save; the money was already allocated.

I ensured the account remained easily accessible for emergencies so I could draw on it if needed, but avoided mixing it with the funds I used for routine costs. This separation also gave me mental clarity: the balance in that account represented my growing cushion, visible and untouchable for casual spending.

You can do the same by creating a sub-account or a separate account with your bank or digital wallet. Label it clearly as either 'emergency' or 'goal savings.' Isolating these funds reduces temptation and reinforces that they serve a specific purpose, not every day desires.

Link to Goals. Each time I made a deposit, I reminded myself why I was saving: whether it was to build an emergency reserve, prepare for a course of study, or plan a future project.

I gave each savings bucket a name: "Emergency Cushion," "Education Fund," or "Project Seed" so that every contribution connected to a clear intention. This practice transformed abstract numbers into meaningful steps toward something I cared about.

I felt motivated when I saw the balance grow because I understood the impact: this cushion would provide security or enable a planned initiative. For your savings, identify what matters most and assign labels accordingly. Linking deposits to goals helps you cultivate a sense of purpose every time money is deposited into that account. It shifts saving from a dry routine into an act of progress toward your priorities, making it easier to maintain consistency.

Review Periodically. I set reminders every few months to revisit my budget and savings targets. When my income changed through a raise, side work, or altered expenses, I recalculated what percentage I could now allocate without stress. Similarly, if new obligations arose, I adjusted to ensure that saving remained realistic.

These periodic reviews kept my plan aligned with life's changes rather than letting it become outdated. During each review, I asked, 'Is the current percentage still appropriate?' Can I increase it modestly? Do my goals need revising or reprioritising?

I stayed proactive rather than reactive by treating saving as a dynamic practice. You can adopt this rhythm by scheduling quarterly or semi-annual check-ins. Review your cash flow, assess upcoming commitments, and determine whether to adjust or temporarily suspend the savings rate. This ongoing attention ensures that saving continues to align with your situation and evolves in tandem with your financial path.

In faith tradition, "pay yourself first" can be seen as preparing to serve others and honour God, ensuring we have resources to give generously or meet unplanned needs.

Reflection Questions:

- ⌘ Am I consistently saving, or do I only save when I have 'extra' money?
- ⌘ What would happen if an unexpected financial emergency hit me today?

Build an Emergency Fund: I recall vividly the lessons my mother taught about preparing for uncertainty. She would keep a small cache of cash under a tablecloth by her bedside, reminding me never to spend every franc so that we always had something for a rainy day.

During times of conflict, we even hid money outside the door beneath a heavy rock so that whoever returned would find at least a bit of savings intact if danger came. Those experiences taught me that an emergency fund is more than a financial cushion; it is peace of mind and a key to survival planning.

I began my emergency fund with that same spirit: treating each deposit as a safeguard against seasons when income might falter or unexpected costs arise.

An emergency fund should be accessible yet separate from daily spending. I opened a dedicated savings account solely for emergencies, ensuring I would not be tempted to use it for routine expenses. When I first set a goal, I aimed to cover one month's living costs; this initial milestone felt achievable and offered immediate relief when small shocks occurred.

Over time, I increased the target to three months' expenses as my circumstances allowed. Treating the fund as sacred, only for true emergencies, helped maintain discipline. Whenever I tapped into it, I refocused on rebuilding it promptly, reinforcing the habit and preserving the cushion for the next unexpected need.

Studies and widely accepted guidelines suggest aiming for three to six months of essential expenses in a liquid account. This range accounts for varying income stability and personal circumstances. When choosing my target, I considered factors such as variable income streams, potential medical costs, and family responsibilities.

While I did not anchor rigidly to a formula, having a guideline helped me measure progress and stay motivated. It also informed decisions about how quickly to build the fund: during seasons of greater stability or windfall bonuses, gifts, or side-income gains, I directed extra resources toward the emergency cushion rather than spending them immediately.

Maintaining liquidity is key. I kept the emergency savings in an account that earned a modest return but remained easily accessible, so I never hesitated when a genuine need arose. At the same time, I avoided mixing those funds with everyday accounts, seeing the balance separate reinforced its purpose.

I drew from that account without panic when an urgent expense arose, whether it was a medical bill, an urgent repair, or a gap between pay checks. Afterwards, I reprioritised rebuilding it, often automating transfers to restore the balance gradually. This cycle of use and rebuild normalised the practice and strengthened my resilience.

Anticipating possible emergencies can help reduce stress when they occur. I practised "scenario thinking," reflecting on what situations might deplete the fund, such as a sudden health expense, an income interruption, or a major home repair. For each, I considered how much I would need and what steps I would take to replenish afterwards.

This preparation turned vague worries into concrete plans. When a real emergency arose, having thought it through beforehand meant I acted calmly: I knew which categories to adjust and how to redirect resources back into the fund after using them. Discussing these scenarios with my spouse or a trusted friend provided additional clarity and accountability, preventing us from drifting when unforeseen events occurred.

Psychological readiness matters as much as the balance itself. In my journey, seeing the emergency fund grow month by month gave me the confidence to face uncertainties without fear. I celebrated milestones, first reaching one month's expenses and then three months, recognising that each increment represented greater stability.

When setbacks forced a withdrawal, I resisted discouragement by viewing it as evidence that the fund was serving its purpose. I reminded myself that rebuilding was part of the process. This mindset, treating the fund as a living tool rather than a static goal, kept me engaged and reduced anxiety about financial shocks.

Financial planning also involves knowing when to pause the growth of the emergency fund to address other priorities, such as high-interest debt or pressing family needs. I balanced building the cushion with eliminating costly obligations. If the interest on my debt greatly exceeded what my savings earned, I would sometimes redirect extra funds to accelerate debt repayment, while maintaining a minimum emergency balance to avoid incurring new borrowing.

As debts decreased, I shifted focus back to expanding the emergency reserve. This dynamic allocation required honest assessment of priorities and open communication with family, ensuring that building resilience did not come at the expense of other critical objectives.

Over time, my emergency fund became a foundation for further financial steps. With that cushion in place, I felt secure enough to explore longer-term investments, start side projects, or increase my generosity, knowing I could absorb minor setbacks without undue concern.

The habit of prioritising liquidity also influenced my broader saving and budgeting practices: I automated transfers into the emergency account first, then allocated what remained to other goals. This "pay the cushion first" approach mirrored the "pay yourself first" principle, embedding resilience into my financial rhythm.

General best practice recommends 3–6 months of living expenses; in the early stage, one can focus on achieving one month's worth and then scale.

Below are four major steps you can take:

1. Set milestone goals: target first a small buffer (e.g., one week or one month of expenses) to handle minor disruptions; then build a larger cushion.

2. Allocate windfalls: direct bonuses, gifts, or unexpected income toward the emergency fund rather than spending.
3. Maintain liquidity: Emergency savings should be in an accessible but separate account (e.g., high-yield savings), and avoid tying up in long-term investments.
4. Replenish after use: if the emergency fund is used, prioritise rebuilding it.

In summary, building an emergency fund is an act of stewardship and foresight. Drawing on early lessons of hiding cash for safety, saving under uncertain conditions, and blending them with disciplined account separation, guideline-based targets, scenario planning, psychological preparedness, and balanced prioritisation, I cultivated a robust cushion that underpins my financial stability.

Treat each deposit with peace of mind. Learn that true financial resilience arises from having resources and the habit of preparing thoughtfully, using the fund wisely when needed, and rebuilding it intentionally.

Think Beyond Today

Saving goes beyond protecting against immediate shocks; it becomes a means to prepare for life stages I could barely imagine at the outset. Reflecting on my upbringing,

I recall how my mother and sister made sacrifices so that I could attend a better school, which instilled in me the value of planning ahead. When I learned that even small deposits for a young child could grow substantially over the years, I opened accounts early for my children, trusting that time would work in our favour.

Identifying milestones, such as education, homeownership, and family formation, led me to establish savings structures way before those seasons arrived, so each contribution felt like an investment in their future.

Thinking about my later years reinforced this outlook. I recalled lessons about keeping resources hidden for emergencies and recognised that planning must account for ageing and potential health needs. I opened long-term accounts for retirement and health-related expenses, treating each deposit as peace of mind for myself and my loved ones.

Although I could not predict exactly how circumstances would unfold, building a foundation reduced the burden on the family if challenges arose. Each transfer into those accounts became an act of responsibility, aligning daily discipline with a vision of security in uncertain times.

I created distinct "buckets" to shape long-term savings tied to specific goals and timelines. For my children's education, I contributed regularly to an account and encouraged them, as they grew older, to add what they could so they'd learn the saving habit firsthand.

For retirement, I automated transfers, so contributions happened without needing constant attention. For other aspirations, buying a home, launching a side project, or supporting a cause, I designated separate vehicles suited to the horizon and risk involved.

Segmenting goals turned abstract hopes into tangible targets: watching each balance climb motivated me to stay consistent and adjust my contributions as life changed.

Balancing long-term saving with other priorities requires flexibility. There were seasons when paying down high-interest debt or addressing urgent family needs became a priority. During those times, I maintained a minimum balance in long-term accounts, so momentum was not entirely lost; then, I refocused on rebuilding contributions once pressing obligations eased.

This approach prevented me from abandoning my future under pressure; instead, I made prudent adjustments to my contributions, knowing that even modest, steady deposits over time yield results.

As I discovered the benefits of investing beyond simple savings, I studied the basic principles of diversification, understanding fees, and aligning investments with timelines so that funds intended for years ahead could generate growth. At the same time, shorter-term goals remained in liquid, lower-risk vehicles.

I did not chase every market trend; I chose instruments aligned with each objective's horizon. This layered strategy enabled me to capitalise on growth opportunities without exposing essential near-term savings to undue volatility.

Envisioning beyond today also encompassed legacy and generosity. I considered how my accumulated resources could benefit my family, community, or the causes I care about. By integrating planned giving into long-term plans, such as designating portions for future support or creating small endowments, I connected my saving and investing with values that outlast my lifetime. This perspective shifted financial planning into a holistic practice, making it less about amassing wealth and more about stewarding it for the well-being of others and for purposes that endure.

Regular review kept these long-term strategies aligned with evolving realities. Each year, I revisit my goals, checking whether children's plans have shifted, whether career changes warrant adjusting my retirement targets, or whether new opportunities suggest rebalancing my resources.

These check-ins served as milestones to celebrate progress and renew commitment to the next phase.

Treating saving as an evolving practice rather than a fixed plan ensured that my efforts remained purposeful and responsive to life's changes.

Tools for Long-Term Financial Vision.

Several practical tools and exercises can prompt readers to extend their financial perspective beyond the immediate moment, as well as life events that naturally trigger long-term thinking.

Create a visioning exercise or financial timeline by listing anticipated life stages, career milestones, family additions, home purchase, education goals, retirement, health considerations, and legacy plans. Assign approximate dates or age ranges.

Map these future events on paper or in a spreadsheet to shift focus from day-to-day cash flow to the needs and opportunities ahead. Include expected costs (tuition, mortgage down payment, medical expenses) and desired resources (seed capital for a venture, travel funds, philanthropic contributions). Seeing these items laid out encourages planning: work backwards from each milestone, estimating how much to save monthly or annually to meet those targets.

Use a scenario-planning worksheet to deepen long-term thinking. Identify plausible shifts, such as a change in income, an unexpected medical expense, or a chance to invest in a new project and write "if–then" responses.

For example: "If income drops next year, reduce certain discretionary categories and draw on a modest reserve," or "If an opportunity arises to start a side business, allocate a portion of savings to seed capital while maintaining the emergency cushion."

Formalising scenarios ahead of time reduces reactive stress and makes adapting more deliberate. Structure this worksheet in simple columns or a table: list each scenario alongside its corresponding adjustment plan to cultivate preparedness.

Apply a goal-setting framework to translate broad aspirations into actionable steps. Define specific, measurable objectives, "save a set amount for a child's education by age 18" or "build a reserve covering six months of expenses within two years," and break each goal into smaller milestones, such as monthly or quarterly saving targets.

Schedule periodic check-ins, quarterly or semi-annual reviews, to adjust contributions as income or expenses change. Treat saving or investing as a recurring commitment, rather than an optional afterthought, to embed consistency and reinforce a habit of looking ahead.

Leverage digital or analogue tools for tracking and projection. Use a compound-interest calculator (via a spreadsheet formula or an app feature) to show how regular deposits grow over time, making the benefit of starting early tangible.

Employ budgeting or financial planning apps with goal trackers to remind you of progress toward education funds, retirement accounts, or other objectives. Even a handwritten chart on a wall or a vision board with images representing future aspirations can be a visual cue. Observing growth over the months strengthens motivation and makes long-term thinking more natural.

Engage in journaling prompts focused on values and legacy. Reflect on questions such as "What impact do I want to have on my family or community in ten or twenty years? How might financial choices today support that vision?"

Write answers to cultivate a sense of purpose tied to financial planning. Imagine a letter from a future self, describing how disciplined saving or investing enabled specific achievements or contributions. Anchoring abstract goals in personal meaning makes long-term effort feel worthwhile.

Appreciate life situations that push toward future thinking. During major transitions, such as marriage, having children, career shifts, moving to a new location, planning for education, housing, or altered income streams. In health events, personal or family assess reserve and insurance needs.

When encountering an unexpected windfall, decide whether to spend immediately or allocate it toward future priorities. After a financial setback, job loss, or a large unplanned expense, treat it as a wake-up call to reinforce tools like emergency funds and scenario planning. Use these triggers as opportunities to revisit and expand long-term strategies.

Cultivate a mindset of adaptability by treating planning as a dynamic process. Recognise that goals may shift as interests or circumstances evolve, so perform periodic reviews. When a new opportunity arises, such as pursuing further education, launching a venture, or taking on caregiving responsibilities, revisit the financial timeline and adjust contributions or timelines accordingly. Embrace flexibility to prevent paralysis when life changes and maintain focus on overarching objectives rather than only immediate concerns.

Conduct peer or mentor discussions to identify blind spots and generate new ideas. Discuss your future aspirations and explore the financial implications with a trusted friend, family member, or advisor. Such conversations often reveal resources or strategies that are not considered alone. Sharing plans builds accountability:

knowing someone else is aware of long-term goals increases motivation to follow through on saving or investing commitments.

Integrate small experiments to reinforce forward thinking.

Commit a modest portion of income to a long-term goal for a set period, effectively testing how living on the remainder feels before scaling up. Alternatively, simulate the impact of a sudden expense by temporarily diverting a small amount from another fund and observing how to manage it. These trials sharpen awareness of trade-offs and build confidence in handling real scenarios when they arise.

Combine these tools and exercises to map future needs, formalise scenarios, set measurable goals, track visually, reflect on values and legacy, respond to life transitions, engage in supportive conversations, and experiment thoughtfully to develop a resilient mindset oriented toward long-term security and purpose. Use the table of practical tools as a quick reference while applying deeper exercises to sustain a forward-looking stance without losing sight of present responsibilities.

Having explored each tool in depth, a markdown table summarising practical tools for extending the financial perspective is below. It's accompanied by explanatory paragraphs to help you draft one that will serve you effectively.

Tool / Exercise	Description	Purpose	How to Implement
Financial Timeline	A chronological chart of anticipated life stages and associated costs.	Encourage foresight about future needs.	List milestones (education, home, retirement, etc.) with approximate dates; estimate costs and required savings.
Scenario Planning Worksheet	A structured list of "if–then" scenarios detailing potential financial shifts and responses.	Reduce reactive stress by predefining responses.	Identify plausible events (income drop, unexpected expense, opportunity); write corresponding

			adjustment plans.
Goal-Setting Framework	Breakdown of long-term objectives into specific, measurable targets and interim milestones.	Translate broad aspirations into actionable steps.	Define targets (e.g., amount for an education fund by a specific date); split into monthly or quarterly saving goals; schedule regular reviews.
Visual Progress Tracker	Charts or trackers (digital or handwritten) showing growth toward savings or investment goals.	Anchor planning in a meaningful purpose.	Answer questions like "What legacy do I want to leave?" Write future-self letters describing outcomes

			of discipline.
Peer/Mentor Discussion	Conversations with trusted individuals about future aspirations and financial implications.	Surface blind spots, generate ideas, and build accountability.	Schedule a meeting or informal chat, share plans, solicit feedback and support, and revisit discussions periodically.
Life Transition Review	A checklist of recent or upcoming changes (marriage, children, career shifts) prompting plan updates.	Trigger the timely adjustment of long-term strategies to ensure optimal performance.	At each major change, revisit the timeline and goals, and adjust saving targets or timelines to fit the new circumstances.

Compound Growth Illustration	A savings or investment growth model should be used to show how small contributions grow over time.	Make the benefit of early and consistent saving tangible.	Use a simple spreadsheet formula or calculator to project future balances, and review the results to reinforce the habit.
Experimentation Exercises	Small-scale tests of adjustments (e.g., allocating a portion of income to a long-term goal).	Build confidence and reveal trade-offs in a low-stakes manner.	Commit to a modest saving or reallocation for a set period, observe how living on the remainder feels, and refine the plan.

| Periodic Review Schedule | A recurring calendar reminder to check progress and update plans. | Keep strategies aligned with evolving realities. | Set quarterly or semi-annual reminders; during reviews, compare actual results to planned outcomes and adjust contributions or timelines as needed. |

Table No.1: Practical tools for extending financial perspective

Below are suggestions on how to work with this table and integrate the tools:

Begin with the timeline: sit down and map out major life stages you anticipate. Use that as the foundation for goal-setting and scenario planning. Once you have milestones and cost estimates, define specific objectives. (For example, saving a certain amount for a child's education by a target year). Break each objective down into smaller steps that you can track on a monthly basis.

Use the scenario worksheet to prepare for possible shifts. For instance, if you expect a career change or potential health expense, outline how you would adjust spending or draw on reserves in writing. When you discuss these scenarios with a mentor or spouse, you refine the responses and reinforce commitment.

Maintain a visual tracker to monitor your progress. Whether it's a simple line graph or a table in a notebook, updating and observing growth helps sustain motivation. Pair this with periodic reviews: schedule times in your calendar to revisit goals, check actual savings against targets, and adapt plans when income or needs change.

Mirror through journaling on how each tool aligns with your values and legacy. Writing about why you want a certain fund or what impact you hope to achieve makes the work more meaningful. Share key plans with a trusted peer or mentor: their feedback can reveal blind spots and bolster your resolve.

When life transitions occur, such as marriage, children, or relocation, use the checklist to trigger updates: revise timelines and saving targets to remain realistic. To reinforce confidence, try small experiments: commit a bit more toward a long-term goal for a month or two and observe how it affects your spending. These trials sharpen awareness of trade-offs and demonstrate your capacity to adapt.

When these tools are combined in a cohesive process, mapping future needs, planning scenarios, setting measurable goals, tracking visually, reflecting on values, engaging support, and reviewing regularly, you cultivate a forward-focused mindset.

The table serves as a quick reference, allowing you to adapt each exercise to your specific situation. Use it as a guide to build and sustain long-term financial vision and resilience.

Ultimately, envisioning beyond today meant setting clear targets, allocating education funds, securing retirement, and establishing legacy intentions, while accepting that life can take unexpected turns. Automating contributions, segmenting goals, learning about appropriate saving and investment vehicles, and periodically reviewing plans, builds a framework honouring current responsibilities and future possibilities.

Each deposit represents faith in tomorrow's potential and the stewardship of resources entrusted to us. Through this approach, saving evolves into a lifelong practice of hope, responsibility, and intentional generosity.

> **Action Step:**
> Start by **saving a fixed percentage of your income,** even if it's just **5-10%**. If you don't already have an emergency fund, **commit to saving at least one month's worth of expenses** over the next few months. Open a separate savings account if you haven't already done so.

Conclusion

Treating saving as an essential practice reshapes the view of money into something purposeful rather than residual. When savings are prioritised, each contribution signals commitment to long-term well-being and creates a foundation for handling unexpected needs.

> *Saving is about how much you keep, not what you earn. Every dollar you save today is a dollar working for your future.*

Discipline in saving fosters patience and trust, making financial decisions align more closely with core values and aspirations without feeling deprived. Consistency in allocating a portion of income to dedicated accounts builds confidence in one's ability to steward resources faithfully.

Establishing saving as a must-pay obligation and revisiting targets as circumstances evolve enables balancing present needs with future goals. This approach strengthens financial self-efficacy and opens pathways for growth, such as pursuing learning, supporting causes, or exploring new opportunities, knowing a reliable cushion is in place.

View saving as an act of responsibility and hope. Allow each deposit to reinforce the belief that stability and flexibility can coexist. Embrace the discipline of saving to ground decisions, prioritise what matters most, and extend support when needed. In doing so, a robust reserve becomes more than just funds; it becomes resilience, freedom, and capacity to serve purposes that endure beyond today.

CHAPTER SEVEN

ESCAPING THE DEBT TRAP

"The borrower is slave to the lender."

— Proverbs 22:7 (NIV)

Diagnosing how debt can erode freedom underscores the importance of escaping the debt trap. Observing obligations accumulate against future income reveals the urgency of addressing liabilities decisively. Embracing a path toward debt freedom enables resources to serve meaningful purposes rather than being used to service past obligations.

Drawing on my experience, I can offer guidance on recognising the full impact of debt, implementing disciplined elimination strategies, resisting social pressures, and establishing habits that sustain a debt-free lifestyle.

Considering the True Cost of Debt

Examining debt begins with knowing its impact on well-being. Carrying balances month after month can lead to chronic stress. Financial worry often manifests as restless sleep or persistent tension.

Observing how worry over due dates can distract from daily tasks highlights that debt affects more than the wallet. Stress from obligations can strain health and undermine confidence. Noting these effects clarifies that debt is not just a set of numbers, but a factor that affects both the mind and body.

Opportunity cost reveals another dimension. Money used for debt payments cannot be channelled into saving or investing. Over time, this means missed growth that could have built security or supported ambitions. For example, funds allocated toward interest could have been better utilised in an emergency reserve or a retirement account. Calculating roughly how much it could have grown if directed elsewhere makes the cost concrete. Recognising that each payment of interest delays building a firm foundation shifts repayment from optional to essential.

Behavioural tendencies often perpetuate debt. The pattern of making only minimum payments keeps balances lingering and interest accumulating. Instant gratification can tempt additional borrowing: a small purchase today may lead to extended payments with added interest.

Understanding these tendencies helps to pause before adding new obligations. Tools such as a simple debt calculator or spreadsheet can illustrate how minimum payments stretch out over the years and how extra payments reduce the total cost. Seeing the numbers makes the pattern clear and motivates change.

Relationship dynamics also reflect the cost of debt. Conversations about money can become tense when obligations loom. Trust may erode if one partner feels burdened by the other's borrowing decisions. An open discussion about existing debt, without blame, reveals how obligations impact shared goals and emotional harmony. Noting how debt can limit choices, postpone plans, or create frequent worries underscores why addressing it is a shared concern.

Spiritually, considering freedom and stewardship offers insight. Freedom here means directing resources toward meaningful purposes rather than servicing past commitments. Viewing debt as an obligation that narrows options connects to the values of wise resource management. Reflecting on principles of contentment and responsible planning frames debt elimination as an act of faithful stewardship rather than mere financial prudence.

Risk assessment highlights vulnerability. High debt levels reduce an individual's or a country's resilience in the face of emergencies. An unexpected medical expense or urgent repair may necessitate further borrowing if no financial cushion exists. Recognising that debt amplifies vulnerability encourages building a buffer and tackling obligations swiftly. The debt-to-income ratio is a useful indicator: when a large portion of income goes to payments, little remains for other needs or opportunities. Observing this metric helps gauge the urgency of repayment.

Legal and practical consequences illustrate real costs. Missed payments can result in penalties, damaged credit, higher future borrowing costs, asset repossession, or legal action. These outcomes carry a financial loss and an emotional toll, characterised by uncertainty and regret. A personal account from the transcript described a relative facing asset loss due to payments falling behind. That experience clarified how quickly obligations can cascade into hardship if left unaddressed.

Social influences shape borrowing behaviour. Pressure to match peers in lifestyle or celebrations can drive decisions that lead to debt. Recognising how external expectations feed borrowing helps to question whether purchases align with genuine priorities. Noting that fulfilling social norms at the expense of financial health often causes regret reinforces the need to align spending choices with long-term well-being.

Understanding the cumulative effect of small debts is also important. Even modest balances with moderate interest add up when multiple obligations coexist. Adding all balances into one view reveals how scattered debts combine into a heavy load. First-person reflection on listing every liability, credit facilities, small loans, and informal borrowings brings clarity. Seeing all obligations together transforms vague anxiety into a clear plan: this is what must be addressed first.

Emotional relief from reducing debt provides motivation. Experiencing the drop in worry when a balance is paid off illustrates how each repayment builds momentum. That feeling of relief reinforces the commitment to continue.

Reflecting on earlier seasons when a small extra payment freed up mental space shows how progress affects finances and mood. Recognising that relief is part of the true benefit encourages perseverance.

Finally, understanding the true cost of debt means viewing repayment not as a punishment, but as reclaiming freedom. Each payment shifts resources from past obligations toward present priorities. Framing elimination as an investment in choices, saving, giving, and exploring opportunities recasts the process in a positive light. Combining personal lessons with awareness of stress, opportunity cost, behavioural traps, relationship effects, risk, and social factors deepens understanding and fuels decisive action.

Steps for Eliminating Debt

Approaching debt elimination with a clear mindset lays the foundation for reclaiming financial freedom. The following steps outline a path to address obligations decisively, build consistent habits, and support lasting stability. These actions guide a structured process that transforms repayment from a burden into an empowering practice.

Listing every obligation in one place brings clarity.

Begin by writing down each balance owed on credit accounts, personal loans, and informal borrowings, along with the interest rate and minimum payment. Seeing all obligations together turns vague worry into a concrete plan, enabling effective prioritisation rather than guessing which debts to address first.

Choosing a repayment approach depends on motivational and cost considerations.

One option balances the highest interest to reduce the total cost over time. Another targets smaller balances first to achieve quick wins that build momentum. Either approach succeeds when applied consistently.

For example, focusing on the highest interest debts frees up more budget later, while closing small balances offers psychological encouragement. Select the path that aligns best with your temperament and adjust as progress unfolds.

Improving the budget supplies resources for extra payments.

Review your monthly expenses to identify areas where modest changes can lead to significant savings. Simplifying meals at home, reducing subscription costs, and delaying nonurgent purchases creates additional money to direct toward debt.

Automate these extra payments so transfers occur without repeated decisions. Consistency overcomes the temptation to revert to old spending habits and steadily accelerates repayment.

Evaluating negotiation or refinancing opportunities requires careful judgment.

Lowering the interest rate or shortening the repayment period can speed up elimination. Extending the term for a slightly lower payment may prolong the debt repayment period.

Examine each offer by asking whether it shortens the path to freedom without increasing overall cost. Proceed when a better rate results in a shorter schedule and actual savings. Otherwise, maintain focus on paying down the original terms.

Avoiding new obligations is essential while existing debts remain.

Suspend credit card use for nonessential spending and resist taking on new lines of credit. When unexpected needs arise, rely on the emergency fund rather than borrowing again, reinforcing the habit of using savings for true emergencies and preventing balances from creeping upward.

Engaging accountability strengthens commitment.

Share the repayment plan with a trusted partner or mentor. Discussing progress aloud encourages honesty about the effort required. Questions from others prompt refinements in approach and sustain discipline when motivation wanes.

Scheduling regular reviews maintains momentum.

Set monthly check-ins to track remaining balances, note the amount of interest saved through extra payments, and adjust repayment amounts if income or expenses change. Observing totals shrink reinforces confidence and reminds us why our efforts matter. Recording each milestone, closing an account, or reducing total debt by a clear amount, provides tangible evidence of progress and a reminder of the relief ahead.

Celebrating each payoff moment reinforces resolve.

The relief experienced when a balance reaches zero shows how debt elimination affects more than finances. It eases worry, improves sleep, and allows redirecting that payment amount toward savings or giving.

Remembering these benefits sustains motivation when the journey feels long. Each cleared debt serves as proof that disciplined action leads to freedom.

Framing repayment as reclaiming control over resources shifts perspective.

Treat each payment as a step toward greater stability and capacity to invest in meaningful goals. Combine personal experience with sound principles to make elimination a structured journey. With clarity, consistency, accountability, and thoughtful evaluation of refinancing options, the path forward becomes clear and achievable.

Treating repayment as a means to reclaim control over resources shifts the experience from one of obligation to one of empowerment. Embracing a deliberate approach builds confidence in handling finances and reinforces belief in directing money toward meaningful goals. Each decision to address debt demonstrates a commitment to stability and freedom rather than a reluctant duty.

Over time, this mindset creates resilience: challenges no longer trigger panic, but prompt thoughtful responses grounded in prior planning. The true reward lies not merely in eliminating balances but in the restored capacity to choose how income is used for saving, giving, or pursuing new opportunities free from the burden of past liabilities.

Continuous dedication to this attitude transforms repayment into a pathway toward lasting financial well-being.

Reflection Questions:

- ⌘ Am I in control of my debt, or is my debt controlling me?
- ⌘ How much of my income is going toward paying off past decisions instead of building my future?

Cultural and Social Pressures That Lead to Debt

Cultural expectations often create obligations that strain finances without being immediately obvious. In many communities, major life events such as weddings, funerals, naming ceremonies, or religious celebrations carry unspoken norms about scale and expense.

Feeling obliged to meet these expectations drives people to borrow funds or use credit cards even when their budgets cannot support the costs. Observing how such norms vary across regions and social circles underscores that pressure to conform can be subtle yet powerful. Identifying that these expectations stem from shared values about honour, status, or belonging helps to understand why refusing or scaling back can be difficult.

Social comparison further intensifies the urge to spend beyond one's means. Witnessing friends or acquaintances exhibit certain lifestyles on social media or in person can foster the perception that similar spending is necessary to belong. The desire to fit in or to appear successful can override budgeting instincts. In my experience, noticing peers upgrade their possessions or host elaborate gatherings led to the temptation to match those standards. Reflecting on how fleeting satisfaction from such purchases contrasted with long-term cost clarified that social comparison often drives decisions misaligned with personal goals. This dynamic shows how easily credit can bridge the gap between reality and perceived expectations.

Among the fundamentals of personal finance is debt management, but managing it effectively is crucial for achieving financial stability. Understanding the various types of debt, their implications, and how to manage them effectively enables us to make informed decisions and avoid financial pitfalls.

There are two main types of debt: good debt and bad debt. Good debt is an investment that will grow in value or generate long-term income. Examples include student loans, mortgages, and business loans. These types of debt are considered good because they contribute to our financial growth and stability.

Bad debt, on the other hand, is incurred to purchase things that quickly lose value and do not generate income. Examples include credit card debt, payday loans, and car loans. Bad debt can quickly accumulate and lead to financial strain if not managed properly.

Family dynamics also play a role. In many cultures, extended family networks expect members to contribute to group activities or provide support during difficult times. When requests arise to contribute to communal funds or assist relatives in need, individuals may tap into their savings or incur debt.

While generosity and solidarity are of great importance, these obligations can sometimes exceed personal capacity. Experiencing instances where aiding a family member required borrowing underscored the tension between caring responsibilities and personal financial stability. Recognising that cultural norms regarding reciprocity and support can lead to debt highlights the importance of striking a balance between generosity and sustainable limits.

Marketing and consumer culture reinforce pressure to spend. Constant exposure to advertising messages suggests that new product experiences or lifestyles are essential for happiness or acceptance. The belief that purchasing items will bring status or improve well-being can lead to impulsive buying financed by credit.

Noticing how advertising taps into desires for identity expression or social approval reveals why resisting debt impulses requires awareness of these influences. Recognising that consumption patterns shaped by marketing may conflict with deeper values helps to prevent unplanned borrowing.

Psychological factors underlie these pressures. The need for belonging, status, or approval can drive spending behaviours. The fear of missing out may prompt participation in activities that exceed one's budget.

Emotional triggers, such as insecurity, loneliness, or the desire for acceptance, influence spending, which helps explain why debt is accumulated during certain seasons. Awareness that emotions often influence financial choices underscores the importance of examining motives before engaging in costly social rituals or making purchases. These internal drivers clarify the roots of borrowing decisions.

Cultural rituals can require significant outlays. Traditions such as dowry, bride price, or ceremonial gifts have deep symbolic meaning and carry community importance. The expectation to honour these customs can lead to substantial expenses. In some contexts, meeting these costs is seen as a measure of respect or honour for family or community members. Witnessing how individuals felt shame or risked social standing if unable to meet these expectations demonstrated that cultural obligations may push people into debt. Understanding the meaning behind these rituals and exploring ways to honour tradition within means can prevent excessive borrowing.

Technology and social media amplify the visibility of others' lifestyles, creating a constant environment for comparison. The impulse to display one's life through curated images or keep pace with perceived norms can lead to purchases financed by borrowing. Reflecting on moments when scrolling through social feeds sparked desires I could not afford revealed how digital environments fuel spending impulses. Recognising the link between online comparison and debt accumulation clarifies why conscious habits around media consumption matter for financial health.

Peer influence often extends to group spending in social activities. Agreeing to dine out at expensive venues or joining group trips can involve costs that exceed individual comfort.

Declining invitations may risk social friction; however, participating can entail using credit to cover expenses. Recalling times when I felt obligated to join peers despite budget constraints highlighted how group dynamics drive borrowing. This pattern emphasises that social cohesion sometimes comes at a financial cost and encourages scrutiny of which activities align with one's values.

Economic transitions, such as migration or changes in income levels, also affect perceptions of appropriate spending. When moving to a new environment where the cost of living is higher or social norms differ, people may feel pressure to adjust their spending patterns to align with local standards.

Throughout my journey, adapting to new contexts required striking a balance between the desire to fit in and the need to live within one's means. Adjustment periods can trigger debt if not managed consciously, and help plan for these transitions to avoid borrowing and appear established.

How to Resist Cultural and Social Pressures

Resist cultural and social pressures by *clarifying your values and priorities*. Ponder what matters most in life and finance, then compare your spending impulses against those core principles.

When faced with expectations for costly events or purchases, take a moment to consider if they align with those priorities. This awareness makes it easier to decline or scale back plans without feeling guilty.

Establish clear boundaries and communicate them to others. Explain that prioritising family needs or building stability precedes meeting every social expectation. Suggest meaningful alternatives, such as gathering in a simple setting or offering a thoughtful yet modest gift. Presenting choices as responsible care rather than a refusal to celebrate fosters understanding and respect.

Create a modest social budget within overall planning. Allocate a limited amount for social activities so that connection remains possible without excess. Once that fund is used, opt for low-cost or free ways to engage. This practice honours relationships while preventing unplanned borrowing.

Cultivate gratitude and contentment to counter comparison. Regularly note aspects of life that bring satisfaction independent of spending. When social media or peer activities trigger the desire to match others, recall past moments of joy that cost little. This mindset reduces the urge to borrow to keep up.

Limit exposure to triggers. Reduce time spent scrolling through images that spark spending impulses. Choose media or conversations that reinforce prudent habits. When group plans threaten to exceed budget, suggest alternatives that fit within means or propose sharing costs in ways that do not rely on credit.

Build supportive networks focused on shared financial goals. Discuss challenges and successes with friends or mentors who respect boundaries. Collective encouragement makes it easier to stand firm when pressure mounts. Mutual accountability can include joint saving goals or simple gatherings reinforcing the choice to spend thoughtfully.

Plan for predictable cultural events. Identify upcoming ceremonies or transitions and decide in advance how to participate within budget. Setting spending limits and choosing modest contributions prevent last-minute borrowing. Preparing alternatives or gradual saving for known obligations reduces stress when the occasion arrives.

Examine motivations before spending. Notice whether the desire to impress or avoid judgment drives choices. Question whether an expense serves a genuine connection or merely addresses insecurity. This reflection supports decisions rooted in authenticity and long-term well-being.

When adapting to new environments or changes in income, strike a balance between fitting in and living within your means. Distinguishing outward appearances matters less than stability and purpose. Prioritise gradual adjustment over sudden spending to appear established.

Combining clarity on values, clear communication, a modest social budget, gratitude practices, controlled exposure to triggers, supportive peer groups, event planning, and motivation checks makes it possible to resist pressures that lead to debt. These steps protect stability and enable resources to serve meaningful goals rather than social expectations.

Creating a Debt-Free Lifestyle

Reaching zero balances marks a transformative moment, but sustaining freedom requires embedding new habits into daily life. Building a cushion for unexpected expenses prevents the need to resort to borrowing when surprises arise.

I prioritised setting aside small monthly amounts into a reserve separate from other savings. When an unplanned cost arose, I drew from that cushion and then focused on rebuilding it promptly. Over time, this practice made relying on credit for emergencies feel unnecessary and strengthened confidence in handling financial shocks without incurring new obligations.

Maintaining disciplined budgeting and saving practices keeps resources aligned with priorities rather than obligations. I continued tracking income and expenses in a journal and updated the plan whenever circumstances changed. This habit revealed when spending drifted toward nonessential items and allowed adjustments before pressures mounted.

Regular budget reviews ensured that funds previously devoted to debt payments could be redirected toward more meaningful goals, such as supporting family projects or investing in personal development. Treating budgeting as an ongoing conversation rather than a one-time task reinforced stability.

Cultivating contentment fosters restraint and reduces the inclination to borrow for unnecessary wants. Dazzling on simple pleasures and recalling times when modest choices brought deep satisfaction helped me resist the urge to accumulate beyond what I needed.

In seasons when social comparison tempted me to spend, I paused to list things I already appreciated. That practice diffused impulses and reminded me that genuine well-being arises from experiences and relationships rather than material displays. Embracing contentment became a cornerstone of a debt-free outlook.

Planning for known future expenses prevents sudden shortfalls that can trigger borrowing. I identified periodic costs, such as vehicle maintenance or seasonal needs, and created sinking reserves to cover them.

Saving a small amount each month for these anticipated outlays meant I never faced urgent decisions funded by credit. This forward-looking approach transformed potential crises into manageable events, keeping the path clear of new liabilities.

Expanding income options bolsters resilience and accelerates progress beyond debt elimination. Drawing on lessons about diversifying income, I explored side activities that aligned with my skills and interests. The additional funds provided flexibility to increase contributions to savings or support community causes without compromising core stability.

When primary income fluctuated, these alternatives served as buffers, preventing the need to turn to credit. Cultivating multiple income streams became a habit that reinforced financial security and opened growth opportunities.

Embedding generosity within means affirms that giving can coexist with prudence. After clearing all debts and establishing a stable cushion, I allocated regular amounts to help others. Experiences of assisting family members in moments of need demonstrated how resources once tied up in debt could now flow toward supporting loved ones. This act of sharing reinforced the value of freedom from obligation and deepened a sense of purpose. Generosity became an integral part of the debt-free lifestyle, rather than a separate goal.

Regular reflection on the journey reinforces commitment to lasting habits. I reminded myself of the relief felt when the final payment posted and observed how resources formerly directed to interest now served constructive aims. These motivated me to maintain discipline even when new challenges appeared. Embracing flexibility ensured that the methods adapted as life evolved. If priorities shifted or new responsibilities emerged, I adjusted the budget and savings plan without losing sight of the debt-free mindset.

Cultivating a supportive environment strengthens resilience. Conversing with trusted peers or mentors about maintaining a debt-free life offered fresh perspectives and encouragement. Sharing successes and challenges created accountability and reinforced determination when pressure arose. Surrounding myself with people who valued responsible resource management fostered a culture where sustaining freedom felt natural rather than exceptional.

Viewing each financial decision through the lens of a debt-free lifestyle transforms choices. Before any purchase, I considered its long-term impact on freedom and opportunities.

This mindset made it easier to decline offers that risked slipping back into debt and prioritise actions supporting stability. Over time, this perspective became intuitive: spending decisions aligned with enduring goals without feeling restrictive.

Creating a debt-free lifestyle combines disciplined planning, ongoing review, contentment, diversified income, intentional generosity, reflective practice, supportive relationships, and a forward-looking mindset. These elements work together to sustain freedom from past liabilities and to direct resources toward meaningful purposes. Implementing this way of living transforms financial habits into practices that cultivate resilience and enable the pursuit of aspirations unburdened by debt.

> **Action Step:**
> Write down **every debt you owe**, including credit cards, loans, and money borrowed from others.
> Choose a **debt repayment strategy,** either the **snowball method** (paying off the smallest debts first for motivation) or the **avalanche method** (paying off the highest-interest debts first to save money).
> **Commit to paying more than the minimum on at least one debt starting this month.**

Conclusion

Treating debt elimination as an act of stewardship transforms the relationship with money from an obligation to empowerment. Adopting a mindset that views each repayment as a reclaiming agency over resources builds confidence in handling future challenges.

Discipline in addressing liabilities fosters resilience and encourages proactive planning in all areas of finance. This perspective shifts attention from past burdens to present choices and future possibilities.

> *Debt is not a life sentence; you have the power to break free. The sooner you take control of your debt; the sooner you'll have full control over your money and your future.*

Cultivating a debt-free mindset nurtures the freedom to direct income toward meaningful goals, such as saving, investing, or giving. Maintaining habits of review, contentment, and adaptable planning ensures stability even as circumstances change.

Embedding generosity within a stable foundation reinforces purpose and the value of responsible resource management. Ultimately, the true lesson lies in the capacity to choose how resources serve long-term well-being once obligations no longer dictate options. Continuous dedication to this attitude sustains financial health and allows one to pursue aspirations without the weight of past liabilities.

PART III

BUILDING WEALTH WITH WISDOM

CHAPTER EIGHT

CREATING MULTIPLE STREAMS OF INCOME

"Invest in seven ventures, yes, in eight; you do not know what disaster may come upon the land."

—Ecclesiastes 11:2 (NIV)

In a world where economic stability can be shaken by a sudden illness, global downturn, or a company restructuring overnight, the wisdom of Ecclesiastes 11:2 rings louder than ever.

This verse isn't merely ancient advice; it's a timeless financial principle that calls for prudence and foresight. Building wealth is about creating sustainability in uncertain times. Multiple streams of income are not about chasing hustle culture; they're about living wisely, protecting your household, and positioning your money to grow with purpose.

When I think about how far God has brought me, especially in terms of finances, one lesson has become crystal clear: relying on a single source of income is a perilous strategy. Life is unpredictable. You never know what storm may hit next.

That's why this scripture from Ecclesiastes is so personal to me. It teaches us to prepare, not in fear, but in wisdom. Diversifying our income is more than a financial strategy; it's a lifestyle of stewardship and foresight.

This chapter explores how I've applied that principle in my own life and how you can start creating multiple streams of income that benefit your household and future generations.

Creating additional income isn't just for entrepreneurs or high achievers. It's for parents trying to fund their children's education, immigrants building a new life, or retirees seeking peace of mind. The concept is simple: the more legs a table has, the stronger it stands. Let's explore how you can add those legs to your financial foundation without compromising your health, faith, or family.

Relying on One Source of Income is Risky

There was a time when I feared leaving my job. I had the benefits, the regular paycheck, and the security of knowing when my next income would arrive. I also felt the weight of being dependent.

I recall a specific instance when I requested a day off for jury duty. I followed the procedure, even emailed my supervisors, but instead of support, I met resistance. That moment opened my eyes. And many other incidents, such as being late for a doctor's appointment by less than an hour, while my colleague is informed. I realised I didn't want to keep explaining myself or seeking permission to live my life. So, I left.

It was not an emotional decision; it was a turning point. I was tired of tying my whole life and well-being to a job that did not allow me to breathe. I knew I could do something for myself. And when I did, I found not only financial freedom, but emotional peace. I started working for myself and began earning more than I had at my structured job.

When we rely on a single stream of income, we place our entire future at the mercy of one employer, one contract, or one health condition. What if something changes? What if your health fails? What if you need time off and your job becomes a burden instead of a blessing?

My independence didn't come overnight, but it began with the courage to believe I was capable of standing on my own two feet. And when I look back, I thank God that I did. He gave me the strength, the wisdom, and the support I needed to break free from financial dependence.

Traditional thinking often encouraged people to pursue a single, stable job and remain with it for their entire careers. For decades, this may have seemed like the safest route. Nevertheless, the economic shifts of the modern world, including job automation, shifting industries, rising living costs, and unpredictable global events, have revealed the fragility of relying on a single paycheck.

When all of your financial provision is tied to one employer or one business, any disruption to that source places your entire livelihood at risk. Building financial resilience requires multiple channels, ones that are not tied to the same source or industry.

This principle is deeply rooted in the Bible's view of stewardship. Throughout Scripture, God rewards those who are productive with what they've been given. The servant who buried his one talent out of fear lost even what he had, while the one who invested and multiplied was given more. Wisdom teaches us to prepare ahead of a crisis, to anticipate seasons of drought by sowing into different fields.

Multiple income streams create room for flexibility, resilience, and growth. They provide options when your environment changes. They also open the door for increased giving, investment, and peace of mind. This is why, through my state-issued license as a financial professional, I am authorised to encourage and educate families and small businesses to establish an income replacement account.

Identify Your Skills and Income Opportunity

I learned early in life that you don't wait for the perfect job or ideal conditions to earn. You look around you, you look within you, and you get creative. "The hero is in you."

When I was a student in the Philippines, far from home and without a sponsor, I had to think quickly. I needed money for textbooks, not a luxury, but a necessity. So, I bought carrots from a nearby farm and sold them to fellow students. I didn't stop there. I knew how to type, so I helped graduate students with their term papers and dissertations. I even made soya milk and sold it to health-conscious friends.

None of these income streams were grand or permanent. They didn't come with business plans or glossy packaging, but they served me and provided for my needs. More importantly, they reminded me that I wasn't helpless. I had options. I had skills. And I had the will to act.

Many people overlook what they already have. They wait for a degree, a license, or someone else's approval before they consider themselves worthy of earning. Nonetheless, skills come in many forms. Some are learned through school. Others are inherited through culture and community. Some you gain through hardship and necessity. My crocheting skills once paid for my son's summer camp. Today, I am grateful for the driving skills that have been supporting my financial needs for more than five years.

I was raised by a mother who farmed, made baskets, did embroidery, hand sewing, managed money with intention, and taught me to cook, clean, and work hard. I also had sisters who taught school during the day, sewed dresses at night, and still found time to farm. That was my classroom. I didn't have to be taught about income diversification in a lecture. I lived it.

You may not see yourself as an entrepreneur, but if you've ever solved a problem, helped someone with a task, or created something others admire, you already hold potential income within you. The United States, with all its complexities, also offers immense opportunities. Whether through the gig economy, digital platforms, or local services, there are ways to monetise your time, talents, and knowledge.

The Bible reminds us that God gives each of us gifts not for decoration, but for use. "Each of you should use whatever gift you have received to serve others" (1 Peter 4:10, NIV). When you serve with your skills, compensation often follows.

So, start where you are. Don't wait for perfection. Make a list of what you're good at. Reflect on what others consistently ask you for help with. Explore how that could become a small stream of income. You may find, as I did, that survival leads to discovery and discovery to purpose.

Reflection Question:

- ⌘ If I lost my primary source of income today, how long could I sustain my current lifestyle?

- ⌘ Am I relying too much on one paycheck?

Making Money Work for You

Growing up, my mother had a unique way of teaching us about money. She didn't sit us down with charts and budgets; nevertheless, she showed us through action. She kept cash in a specific place under a tablecloth near her bed.

When she sent us to get money for something, she always said, "Don't finish it. Save some for when someone needs to go to the dispensary." That simple instruction stayed with me. She was reminding us that money isn't just for spending, it's for preparing.

That mentality shaped how I later approached money as an adult. For many years, I worked hard, earned my income, and spent it responsibly. Eventually, I came to realise that working hard is not enough.

If every dollar you earn depends on your energy, your time, and your physical presence, then you are constantly at risk. What happens when you can no longer work?

What happens when your energy runs out or your situation changes?

That's when I began to understand a deeper principle: money should also work for me.

There is a major difference between earning money and growing money. Earning money is what most people do through jobs or side hustles. Growing money means putting it in vehicles that generate income on their own. This includes savings accounts with high interest, investments in indexed accounts, real estate, digital products, or other tools that produce returns even when you're not actively working.

When I began my journey in financial education, I learned about indexed universal life insurance accounts that not only protect your family in the event of death but also offer *living benefits*. These include tax-advantaged growth, income protection during illness, and financial flexibility when you need it most.

It was a revelation for me. I realised how many families, including those in immigrant communities, suffer not because they lack income, but because their income is not protected or growing.

When I began educating others, I realised how many people were unaware that these options even existed. That's why I take time with each client to explain, not just sell. I conduct a comprehensive Human Needs Analysis, examining their income, age, health, and goals, before recommending any solutions. I believe finances must be personal, not pressured.

The American financial system can be both a blessing and a trap. Without knowledge, many fall into cycles of consumer debt, over-taxation, and financial vulnerability. But with education and action, you can build wealth slowly, safely, and securely. Money is a tool, not a master. And when managed wisely, it can become your partner in purpose.

Proverbs 13:11 says, "Wealth gained hastily will dwindle, but whoever gathers little by little will increase it" (ESV). That verse reminds me that there's no shame in small beginnings.

The key is to begin. Automate a small amount into savings. Explore investment options. Open an account that earns compound interest. Build an emergency fund. Reinvest your returns. Keep learning.

When you let money work for you, you stop living in constant fear. You sleep better. You plan better. You give more freely. Your life becomes less about survival and more about stewardship. That's not just financial growth. That's spiritual alignment.

Balancing Multiple Streams Without Burnout

I've always been willing to work. Even as a girl, I remember climbing coffee trees on our family's farm, helping with banana harvests, raising cows, collecting manure for the farm and cleaning with excellence under my mother's supervision. That work ethic never left me. I carried it into school, into motherhood, into my time living in five different countries, and into my current calling as a financial educator.

But over time, I had to learn that hard work without balance is dangerous. I've worn high heels and suits to nonprofit jobs that looked elegant but left me drained. I've tried to serve faithfully in systems that were demanding, dismissive, and unappreciative. I stayed for as long as I could until I realised that peace of mind is not optional. It is essential.

When I finally stepped out to build my work, I brought with me both strength and scars. I had to learn how to set limits, listen to my body, and structure my days in a way that honoured both productivity and rest. I no longer wanted to be constantly busy. I wanted to be fruitful.

Building multiple income streams is a beautiful goal. It allows for greater stability, faster debt freedom, and increased generosity. But it can also become a burden if it's not approached with strategy and spiritual wisdom.

Not every opportunity is for you. Not every venture needs your time right now.

In my life, I've chosen to integrate my family into my work. My husband and children help with digital design, seminar preparation, and budgeting tools. We use Excel spreadsheets to plan and track our finances. When I need to travel, we agree on the expenses and responsibilities. This kind of support protects me from overload and reminds me that wealth-building should not separate you from your loved ones.

I've also made choices to live a modest life. I say no to excessive celebrations, luxurious purchases, or financial habits that strain my peace. I don't buy expensive gifts I can't afford. I don't spend on big parties. I choose simple meals when the budget is tight. I journal my expenses daily to track where my money is going. These habits may seem small, but they keep me from drifting into chaos.

In the American system, it's easy to get caught in the race. Hustle culture tells us to work more, sleep less, and prioritise financial gain over family. But God's model is different. In His design, there is a Sabbath. There is rhythm. There is rest.

So, if you're building streams, build slowly. Build strategically. Build in alignment with your calling and capacity. Delegate what you can. Automate what you should. Protect your joy. Protect your home.

Multiple streams are a blessing, but only when you're still standing to enjoy the flow.

> **Action Step:**
> Identify one skill, hobby, or knowledge area that could generate extra income. Research side hustles, freelancing, investing, or passive income opportunities that align with your abilities. Commit to starting a new income stream within the next 30 days, even if it's small.

Conclusion

Looking back at everything I've walked through financially, professionally, and personally, I see that God has always been teaching me to multiply. Whether it was selling carrots for textbooks, typing research papers, or now teaching financial education to others, He was shaping in me a mindset of multiplication, not limitation.

Creating multiple income streams isn't just a strategy for success; it's a key to achieving it. It's a way to honour the wisdom God has given us. It's saying, "I will not wait for life to hand me one door. I will steward the keys I already hold."

One income stream will never be enough in today's world, not with rising costs, not with unexpected illnesses, not with global shifts and economic delays. However, when you utilise your skills, protect your income, intentionally grow your money, and balance your work with wisdom, you step into a life that is not reactive, but proactive.

> *Relying on one source of income is risky, diversification is security. The more ways you create income, the more financial freedom you gain. Start small, stay consistent, and watch your financial options expand.*

The financial system in the United States has its complexities, but it also offers tools for anyone willing to learn and take action. Whether you're new to this country or born into it, the principles are the same: plan, protect, build, and give. There is no age too young and no moment too late to start making your money work for you, instead of the other way around.

I don't share my story to impress anyone. I share it because I know what it means to have nothing and still find a way. I know what it feels like to be limited by status, environment, or language and still choose growth. And I know what it means to build something from the ground up, by God's grace, one obedient step at a time.

So, let me encourage you: don't wait for a crisis to diversify. Don't wait for exhaustion to step back and balance. Don't wait to start saving and investing. Let today be your beginning. Whether you start with your time, your hands, your wisdom, or your income, start.

And as you build, remember this: money is a tool. It can either control you or it can serve your God-given purpose. Let it serve your peace, your family, your community, and the next generation. Let it reflect wisdom, faith and freedom.

Because financial freedom is not the absence of work, it's the presence of options. And when you have options, you have the power to choose peace, purpose, and legacy.

CHAPTER NINE

INVESTING FOR THE FUTURE

"The man who had received five bags of gold brought the other five. 'Master,' he said, 'you entrusted me with five bags of gold. See, I have gained five more.' His master replied, 'Well done, good and faithful servant! You have been faithful with a few things; I will entrust you with many things. Come and share your master's happiness!'"

—Matthew 25:20-21 (NIV)

There's something sacred about multiplication. Not just the ability to earn, but the discipline to grow what you've been given.

This parable in Matthew isn't only about gold, it's about mindset. The servant wasn't praised because he worked hard; he was praised because he produced more than what he was entrusted with. He understood that what the master gave him wasn't meant to sit idle; it was meant to increase.

That principle shaped my entire approach to money. I've had to learn, through lived experience, that earning alone won't secure your future. What you do with what you earn is what builds a legacy. That's why investing is not for the rich; it's for the wise. This chapter is about unlocking the door to long-term financial growth and teaching your money to keep working even when you don't.

Investing is the Key to Long-Term Wealth

For most of my life, I believed in the importance of working hard. I worked across cultures, industries, and continents. But over time, I came to understand that smart decisions must accompany that hard work. I saw how families around me were working day and night, yet still retiring broke or dependent. That's when I began learning more intentionally about investing, not as a luxury, but as a necessity.

Investing is what separates short-term income from long-term wealth. It's what allows your money to grow while you sleep. It turns today's dollars into tomorrow's opportunities. And it helps ensure that you are not dependent on your physical strength or monthly salary forever.

Too many of us are raised to think about working for money, but not about how money can work for us. I was raised by people who modelled saving and stretching every coin, but even they did not use the language of investing, because they weren't taught how. We were taught survival, not sustainability.

Yet, investing is what ensures that the money we labour to earn continues to work for us even after we stop working.

In the United States, the financial system is structured in a way that rewards those who invest their money. The wealthy understand this, and that's why they focus on *assets*, not just income. They purchase assets that appreciate over time, such as property, stocks, and business equity. Meanwhile, many ordinary families, especially immigrants, remain stuck working for every dollar because they were never shown how to leverage their resources.

Investing doesn't mean you stop working. It means your money learns how to work *with you*. That's what the servant in Matthew 25 understood. His master gave him money, but he didn't just keep it safe; he multiplied it. And he was praised, not just for his stewardship, but for his boldness to grow what he had been given. That parable is not only about obedience. It's about financial faith.

Let's be honest: the cost of living keeps rising. Groceries are more expensive. Rent and housing prices go up. College tuition and healthcare costs continue to increase annually. If your money sits idle, it loses power. If it is growing, it gives you options. Options to retire early. Options to give generously. Options to take care of your family without borrowing or begging.

One of the most overlooked reasons for investing is the dignity it affords. When you invest and grow your resources, you reduce dependency. You protect your family from sudden shocks. You reduce the chances of needing GoFundMe pages, emergency loans, or last-minute pleas when life's unexpected events occur. It doesn't mean you'll never face hardship; it just means you'll face it with preparation.

That is why I teach families not only how to earn, but how to grow. Because it is not how much money you make that matters, it is how much you keep, grow, and pass on. Whether it's $100 or $1,000, what you do with what you have is what determines your financial legacy.

So, if you want long-term wealth, don't wait for a miracle. Don't wait for a big windfall. Begin to invest. Learn the principles. Seek the guidance. Take small, consistent steps. Because when you do, you're not just building money, you're building freedom.

The Different Types of Investment

When people hear the word "investment," many automatically think of the stock market. The world of investing is much broader than that. Understanding the various types of investments enables you to make informed decisions based on your goals, risk tolerance, and time horizon.

Stock Market Investments

This includes buying shares of companies through platforms like brokerage accounts or retirement accounts (such as IRAs or 401(k)s). Stocks can offer high returns, but they also come with risk. You're essentially buying ownership in a company, hoping it will grow in value and share its profits with you through dividends.

Bonds and Treasury Securities

These are lower-risk investments where you loan your money to a government or corporation in exchange for interest. While they typically grow more slowly than stocks, they offer stability and are often used for preserving capital.

Real Estate

Buying property, whether for rental income or resale value, is another powerful way to build wealth. Real estate often appreciates over time and can provide passive monthly income. However, it requires upfront capital and a thorough understanding of the market.

Index Funds and Mutual Funds

These are bundles of investments that track specific sectors or the overall market. They offer diversification and are ideal for beginners who want steady growth without needing to pick individual stocks.

Retirement Accounts

Tools like Roth IRAs, traditional IRAs, and 401(k)s allow your money to grow with tax advantages. I often teach families how to structure their retirement plans so they can protect their money and access it when it's truly needed without penalties or tax burdens.

Business and Entrepreneurship

Sometimes, the best investment is in yourself or a family business. I've experienced this personally when I chose to start educating people instead of working under pressure for a salary. That decision didn't just free me emotionally; it also multiplied my income and impact.

7. Indexed Universal Life Insurance (IULs)

This is a tool I work with on a regular basis. It offers growth potential based on the stock market index but with protection against loss. It's also tax-advantaged and includes living benefits. For many people, this has become both a safety net and a wealth-building strategy.

Each of these options has pros and cons. That's why it's essential to learn, ask questions, and align your investment with your personal values and life stage. Don't rush. Don't follow hype. Understand what you're doing and why.

Reflection Questions:

- Is my money working for me, or am I the only one working for money?
- What am I doing today to ensure my financial stability in the years to come?

Overcome the Fear of Investing

Fear is often louder than facts, especially when it comes to money. I've sat with families who wanted to build wealth, but fear stopped them from taking the first step.

They feared losing money. They feared being scammed. They feared the unknown. And above all, they feared making a mistake they couldn't recover from.

I remember how I felt the first time I heard someone explain indexed investment products. It sounded foreign, mathematical, even intimidating. Coming from a background where we weren't taught to think of money beyond survival, the word "investment" felt like a language reserved for wealthy people, educated people, and financial insiders. I wasn't sure I belonged in that conversation.

However, I had to remind myself that fear is a natural emotion. It is not a curse, nor is it weakness. It's a signal, an invitation to pause, to ask questions, and to seek knowledge. Fear isn't the enemy. Stagnation is.

The fear of investing often stems from three primary sources: a lack of information, a lack of confidence, and past trauma.

Many of us were raised in environments where money was scarce, risk-taking was discouraged, and financial loss carried significant emotional consequences. So even the idea of "putting money somewhere" instead of holding it tightly can feel like a betrayal of our survival instincts, our upbringing, or our struggle.

That's why the first step to overcoming fear is not opening an account; it's educating yourself with intention. When you begin to learn about terms like compound interest, index funds, dividends, and diversification, they start to lose their intimidation. They become tools instead of threats.

There's also the cultural fear that exists in some immigrant families, especially where financial mistrust has been passed down. I've worked with clients who were told growing up, "Put your money where you can see it."

To them, investing seemed like gambling, rather than a strategy. Others had watched relatives lose their savings in failed schemes, and they developed a deep scepticism about anything involving the stock market or financial products.

The truth is that not investing carries a different kind of risk. The risk of losing value to inflation. The risk of working into old age with no passive income. The risk of having nothing left to pass on. You may not see those risks daily, but they are real and costly in the long run.

That's why I believe overcoming fear also requires redefining what security looks like. Many people think security means having money in a savings account. While savings are important, they rarely grow at a significant rate. True financial security means having a plan for how your money will grow over time and outpace inflation, as well as cover emergencies and future needs.

Investing doesn't require boldness. It requires wisdom. Start small. Understand your risk tolerance. Choose investments that offer protection, like Indexed Universal Life insurance (IULs) or conservative mutual funds. Get professional guidance. Ask questions until you're confident. One of my greatest joys is sitting with clients and watching their fear turn into curiosity and then into bold action.

We must also address the emotional aspect of investing, especially for those who've experienced past financial failures. Some are not afraid of investing; they are afraid of failing again. They carry shame from a business loss, a credit card default, or a bad financial decision.

That shame becomes a wall. To move past it, we must separate the past from the present. You are wiser now. You are not the same person. And God is not holding your past against you. He's inviting you into stewardship.

Scripture reminds us that fear should never have the final say. *"Do not be afraid, little flock, for your Father has been pleased to give you the kingdom"* (Luke 12:32, NIV).

That includes the wisdom, discipline, and courage to grow what He has given you. He is not pleased by the fear that paralyses. He is pleased by faith that takes action.

I always say: if you've been afraid to invest, it means you care. You care about doing it right. You care about protecting your family. That care is not weakness. It's your starting point. Take that care, and add knowledge, prayer, counsel, and small steps of action, and you will see transformation.

Let fear become your teacher, not your master. Ask yourself: *What exactly am I afraid of? And what do I need to know to move forward wisely?* Once you answer that, you're no longer stuck. You're preparing. And preparation is the soil where confidence grows.

Create an Investment Plan that Works for You

When I first began to learn about investments, the language alone made me pause. There were terms I hadn't grown up hearing, such as risk tolerance, diversification, asset classes, and time horizon.

It was humbling to admit that while I was wise in many areas of life, this one still needed growth. And that's where I began by allowing myself to be a student.

Too often, we assume that investing is a one-size-fits-all approach. We think we're supposed to copy someone else's portfolio, jump on popular trends, or follow the latest "hot stock." But true wealth isn't built by mimicking. It's built by planning based on your *values, income, responsibilities,* and *goals.*

Your plan doesn't need to be complicated. It just needs to be clear and consistent. Ask yourself, *"What do I want this money to do for me?"*

Do you want it to grow slowly and safely over time for retirement? Are you saving for your child's education? Do you want to own property in ten years? Are you planning to become financially independent so you can spend more time with your family?

Once you're clear on your goal, you can then determine your time horizon (how long you're willing to wait), your risk tolerance (how much fluctuation you can emotionally and financially handle), and your contribution capacity (how much you can set aside regularly).

Here's what I often teach my clients as a foundational strategy:

- Start with your emergency fund. Ensure you have at least 3 to 6 months of basic living expenses saved in a liquid, readily accessible account.
- Set up automated contributions into your investment or retirement accounts. This makes saving a non-negotiable habit, not a wish.
- Diversify your investments. Don't put everything in one place. Spread it across conservative, moderate, and growth-oriented tools.
- Review your plan at least once a year, or whenever major life changes occur. Marriage, new baby, job change, or a move? Your plan should reflect that.
- Pair your investment plan with protection. This includes insurance tools that shield your family in the event of death, disability, or economic downturns.

Another critical component of a working investment plan is discipline over time. I've seen people start with excitement and stop when life gets busy or the market shifts.

Don't let the headlines guide your decisions. Markets rise and fall; that's part of the process. Stay focused on the long-term goal.

Also, don't underestimate the power of small beginnings. You don't need thousands of dollars to start investing. Even $50 or $100 per month can grow substantially over the years. The key is to start early, stay consistent, and allow your money to work silently in the background while you focus on living.

And finally, your plan should reflect your faith and your values. As believers, we're not just building for ourselves; we're building for a purpose. My investment plan is not only about growth. It's about impact. It's about being able to help family, give to ministry, retire with dignity, and teach my children to think generationally.

So, no matter where you are right now, don't wait until you "have enough." Don't wait for everything to feel perfect. Start with clarity. Start with commitment. And trust that as you move forward, God will guide the increase.

> **Action Step:**
>
> If you haven't started investing yet, **commit to learning about at least one investment option** stocks, real estate, mutual funds, or retirement accounts. If you're already investing, **review your portfolio and set a goal to increase your contributions**. Start with **a small, consistent investment**, even if it's just a few dollars a month.

Conclusion

When I look at my life now, it's hard not to see the fingerprints of wisdom in every financial step I've taken, especially the ones that required faith. I didn't begin with much. I didn't have a blueprint handed to me. I had a desire to grow and a willingness to learn. Over time, those two things became the foundation for everything I've built and everything I now teach others.

> *Wealth isn't built by saving alone it's built by making money work for you. The best time to start investing was yesterday; the next best time is today. Don't wait for the 'perfect time' start now, learn as you go, and secure your future.*

Investing in the future is not a matter of how much money you have; it's a matter of how much you value it.

It's about how much understanding you choose to pursue and how much trust you're willing to place in the process.

God calls us to be good stewards, not just savers. He didn't give us resources so we could bury them in fear. He gave them so we could multiply them with purpose and wisdom.

Wealth doesn't grow by accident. It grows by strategy. It grows by surrendering our fear, confronting our ignorance, and asking for guidance. It grows when we stop living paycheck to paycheck and start living plan to purpose. Your plan doesn't have to be perfect, but it must be active.

If I had waited for full clarity before investing, I might still be stuck in hesitation. Instead, I chose to be faithful with little, and God kept increasing what was in my hand. Not because I knew everything, but because I was willing to be teachable. That same grace is available to you.

The world's financial system may undergo significant shifts. The market may rise and fall. Wisdom remains. Knowledge, applied in faith, has the power to outlast uncertainty. That is why I urge you: don't just think about now. Think generationally. Think eternally. Think with the mindset of a builder, not a consumer.

You are not too late. You are not too old. You are not too behind. Begin now. Invest wisely. Pray intentionally.

And believe that the seeds you plant today will speak for you tomorrow.

Faithful living and smart money management go hand in hand, and both are investments that yield peace, a legacy, and financial freedom.

CHAPTER TEN

FINANCIAL FREEDOM AND GENEROSITY

"Remember this: Whoever sows sparingly will also reap sparingly, and whoever sows generously will also reap generously."

—2 Corinthians 9:6 (NIV)

Money is more than a means to an end; it is a reflection of what we value, how we think, and whom we trust. For many, the pursuit of wealth becomes a chase that never leads to rest. Yet true financial freedom is not about having more, it's about mastering what you have and using it with purpose.

Generosity, often overlooked as a financial strategy, is one of the most powerful forces for sustained increase. When handled with wisdom, both freedom and giving unlock a way of life that is peaceful, impactful, and deeply fulfilling. This chapter explores how to move beyond mere survival and control toward stewardship and liberty, the kind that changes lives, including your own.

Stop Letting Money Control You

Money is meant to serve us, not rule us. It was never designed to be a master. Yet for many, it controls more than just decisions; it shapes identities, defines self-worth, and determines how much joy they allow themselves to feel.

We chase promotions, pack our schedules, and sacrifice our well-being, all in the name of having "enough." Nonetheless, enough never feels like enough when fear is leading the charge.

There's a powerful illusion at work: the belief that money equals control. We tell ourselves that if we can earn more, save more, or invest more, we'll finally feel safe. We convince ourselves that the next raise or the next deal will finally buy us peace of mind. But peace built on a number is fragile. One emergency, market shift, or family crisis can erase what we thought made us secure. In that moment, the illusion shatters.

For immigrants, especially, this illusion often begins with the weight of survival. Having left familiar systems, networks, and sometimes even financial safety nets behind, it's easy to fall into the trap of believing that the only way to reclaim dignity is through relentless financial gain. The pressure to prove ourselves to both others and ourselves can make us idolise money without even realising it.

We say we want freedom, but many are still living in emotional debt. We fear checking our account balances, avoid financial conversations, or judge ourselves harshly for not "having it together." These are signs that money has moved beyond a tool and become a taskmaster.

The truth is that wealth without inner peace is not freedom. It's a heavier chain. A silent, invisible burden that grows even as your bank account does. What good is financial growth if it costs you your health, your joy, or your relationships?

Freedom doesn't come from how much you control; it comes from what you release. It comes from trusting God as your source, not your paycheck. It comes from choosing to let go of the need to impress and embracing a life that reflects your values, not society's expectations.

Real financial freedom starts with this one revelation: *I am not my bank balance. I am not what I earn. I am who God says I am.* And when that becomes your foundation, money loses its power to rule you. You begin to think more clearly, act more intentionally, and give more freely, not out of pressure, but from a place of confidence and trust.

Breaking the Emotional Ties

The journey to financial freedom begins in the heart. Many people fear looking at their bank statements or talking about money at all because it stirs feelings of inadequacy, shame, or regret. These emotions are often associated with childhood, culture, or past experiences of poverty or loss.

To stop letting money control you, it's important to face those fears head-on:

- ⌘ Acknowledge your emotional patterns related to spending, saving, and feelings of scarcity.
- ⌘ Recognise where fear, not faith, has been making your financial decisions.
- ⌘ Replace anxiety with strategy. Emotions may pass, but discipline builds stability.

Redefining Success

True success is not measured by what you own, but by what you're able to walk away from without losing your peace.

This statement challenges everything our culture glorifies. We live in a world that equates visibility with value. The bigger the house, the better the car, the more expensive the wardrobe, the more "successful" we appear. Social media, advertising, and even peer circles constantly push us to measure ourselves by outward symbols of wealth, but all of these can be misleading. You can have a six-figure income and still cry yourself to sleep under the weight of debt, regret, or emptiness.

Success, when defined by society, often leads to comparison and burnout. It becomes a performance rather than a conviction. And when we rely on material achievements to feel validated, we surrender our joy to a moving target. No matter how much you earn or achieve, there's always someone with more. Always another milestone to chase. Always another version of yourself that feels "not yet enough."

But real success, the kind that brings rest, not pressure, is deeply personal and powerfully liberating. It's about alignment, not applause. It's when your life reflects your purpose, your priorities, and your peace. It's when your money supports your values, rather than contradicting them.

You're truly successful when you can:

- ⌘ Leave a high-paying job because it compromises your health or values.
- ⌘ Say no to certain deals because your integrity isn't for sale.
- ⌘ Live below your means because you're building a future, not feeding an image.
- ⌘ Give freely without worrying about scarcity.
- ⌘ Take a break without guilt because you've built your life, not just your bank account.

When you stop chasing money and start directing it, you reclaim your authority. You're no longer at the mercy of comparison or urgency. You become the architect of your life, choosing what fits, discarding what doesn't, and adjusting course as needed without fear of judgment.

This is especially important for those of us who come from backgrounds where success was once defined by survival. When you've fought through poverty, sacrifice, and pressure, it's easy to overcorrect and attach your worth to outward achievement.

Yet, God's definition of success is rooted in stewardship and obedience, not in showing off trophies. It's not about who sees what you have; it's about whether what you have is serving the right purpose.

So, pause and ask yourself: *What does success mean to me?* Strip away the noise. Look beyond what others are doing. Realign with your values. Redefine success on your terms that honour your peace, your faith, and your future.

That is success you can carry with joy, not just in the bank.

Build Wealth with a Purpose

Many people wake up each day, go to work, receive a paycheck, and repeat the cycle month after month, year after year. They are busy, sometimes even successful on paper, yet they feel unfulfilled or stuck. Why? Because there is no vision guiding their finances. They are earning, but they are not building. They are surviving, but not advancing.

Vision is what gives money meaning. Without it, money loses its direction. It gets spent on impulse, wasted on image, or hoarded in fear. But when vision is present, even limited resources begin to stretch with intention and power. You begin to understand that every dollar is a seed, and where you plant it determines your future.

Purpose is not a luxury for the rich; it's a necessity for anyone who desires long-term peace and impact. Vision answers the question: *Why am I working so hard? What is this money meant to accomplish beyond paying bills?*

That clarity is the real asset. Once you know what you're building, you can endure seasons of restraint, make wiser choices, and resist distractions that don't align with your bigger picture.

For some, the vision is retiring early and spending more time with family. For others, it's paying for children's college education debt-free, building a family home, establishing a scholarship fund, or providing consistent support to relatives in their home country.

Some envision opening a business that creates jobs or funding community health initiatives. Whatever your vision is, own it unapologetically and then align your finances accordingly.

Without vision, even a high income will feel like it disappears too fast. You'll wonder where the money went and have little to show for it. With vision, every financial decision becomes part of a larger story, your story. You begin to budget, save, and invest with clarity. You cut unnecessary spending not out of guilt, but out of purpose. You say no to good things because you are committed to greater things.

Vision keeps you focused when you feel tempted to drift. It reminds you that money isn't just about what you can afford now, it's about what you're building for later. And most importantly, vision invites God into your financial plans. It gives you something to pray over, plan for, and steward with excellence.

So, before you chase more income, sit with your values. Define your goals. Visualise the legacy you want to leave behind. When vision leads the way, money becomes a powerful servant and never your master.

From Accumulation to Assignment

There's a profound spiritual shift that occurs when you stop seeing money as a monument to self and start treating it as a servant of purpose. For many, financial growth becomes about arriving, owning more, showcasing more, accumulating for the sake of proof. Yet wealth was never meant to be the end goal. It was meant to be a resource, a vehicle, a tool assigned to serve something greater than itself.

Money without mission becomes noise. It fills our lives with things, but not meaning. It makes us appear full while we feel hollow inside. That's because accumulation, by itself, doesn't satisfy the soul. Only alignment does.

When you begin to assign your money intentionally and prayerfully, you give it direction. Every dollar gets a job. Some dollars are invested to secure your future. Others are tasked with paying down debt. Some are designated to build your business. Others are released to support your church, bless your community, or fund a family member's education. This is financial leadership in action.

An assignment starts with a plan. It shows up in how you budget, not reactively, but with purpose. It shows up in how you give not randomly, but with clarity and generosity. It even shows up in how you spend choosing with discernment, not simply because you can.

This kind of stewardship demands maturity. It means walking past sales when you could swipe your card. It means ignoring trends that don't align with your vision. It means telling yourself the truth: *Just because I can afford it doesn't mean it belongs in my life right now.*

For those of us who have experienced lack, the temptation to accumulate can feel justified. We want to prove that we've made it. We want to reward ourselves. And while there's nothing wrong with enjoying the fruit of your labour, unassigned money often becomes wasted money. It leaks through the cracks of impulse and ego, never fulfilling its higher potential.

Financial peace doesn't come from how much you have; it comes from knowing your money is doing what it was meant to do. And when you begin living that way, you'll find that contentment, clarity, and confidence begin to multiply just as quickly as your resources.

Purpose as the Guardrail

Every road needs a guardrail. Something to keep the vehicle on track, especially when momentum increases. Purpose serves that function in your financial life. It's the invisible but powerful force that keeps you aligned when abundance starts to flow.

One of the most dangerous financial traps is lifestyle inflation, the subtle and almost automatic rise in expenses that accompanies an increase in income. You get a raise, and suddenly a nicer car feels necessary. As your business grows, a bigger home seems justified. Before long, you're earning double what you used to, but saving, giving, and investing less than you should.

Why does this happen? Because without purpose, more income fuels more appetite.

Purpose interrupts that cycle. It reminds you of what you're building, who you're becoming, and what truly matters. It invites you to slow down and evaluate your decisions, not out of fear, but because they are out of alignment with your values. When you know your mission, you can resist the lure of showmanship. You begin to choose sustainability over spectacle, wisdom over flash, stewardship over applause.

Purpose doesn't just guide your spending It guards your soul. It keeps you from defining success in terms of possessions and helps you stay rooted in lasting impact. You begin to think generationally, not just emotionally. You consider what your choices are modelling for your children, your peers, and your community.

As your income increases, purpose becomes the reason you don't drift into waste. It becomes the anchor that holds you steady when comparison tries to sway you. And it becomes the reason your wealth grows with integrity, not just volume.

Kingdom wealth doesn't just look impressive, it works. It serves. It multiplies good. And that only happens when purpose is the guardrail that shapes your every financial step.

Reflection Questions:

- ⌘ Am I financially free, or am I still tied to financial stress and obligations?
- ⌘ How do I view generosity as a burden or as a privilege?

Giving – The Secret to Lasting Wealth

Many people approach giving as an occasional act of generosity, a kind gesture they extend when they feel emotionally moved or when their finances appear stable.

Nevertheless, giving was never meant to be emotional or optional. In the kingdom of God, it is not a side habit. It is a spiritual law. A principle so foundational that it defines how we relate to money, to people, and God Himself.

Giving is not God's way of decreasing what we have. It is His way of teaching us trust, training our hearts in obedience, and positioning us for multiplication. It is not a tax for being spiritual. It is a strategy for aligning with heaven's supply. God does not ask us to give because He needs what we have. He asks us to give because we need to remember that we are not the source. He is.

Each time we give, especially when it stretches us, we proclaim something powerful. We declare that we are not owners, but stewards. We say with our actions that our faith is not in the numbers on a paycheck, but in the faithfulness of a Provider who never runs out. That shift in perspective is not just theological. It is practical. It changes how we make decisions, how we manage increase, and how we pursue wealth.

Too often, people wait to give until they "have enough." In the kingdom, generosity is not based on surplus. It is based on surrender. It is not something we do later; once we arrive, we live by it now, even as we build. God honours that posture. He blesses those who put Him first, not just with spiritual peace but with tangible provision.

When you make giving part of your financial rhythm just as natural as paying bills or saving, you begin to see money differently. You stop clinging. You stop fearing. You live open-handed, confident that what leaves your hand in faith will never leave your life. It will come back multiplied, refined, and purposeful.

Generosity is how we invest in eternity. It is how we contribute to the healing of others while securing favour in our own lives. Whether it is tithing to your local church, giving to a family in need, funding a mission project, or helping someone get through school, your giving plants seeds that will outlive you.

God is not asking for what you do not have. He is inviting you to trust Him with what you do. When you treat giving as a kingdom principle, not a random donation habit, you stop losing money and start sending it on assignment. You become part of God's economy, which does not run dry, crash, or break under pressure.

When you live this way, you do not just become generous; you become a better person. You become free.

Giving Unlocks a Cycle of Increase

Giving is not simply an act of release. It is a declaration of faith that invites a cycle of divine increase. Every time you give with a sincere and willing heart, you break the stronghold of fear and scarcity. You silence the internal voice that tells you to hold back, just in case. You defeat the lie that says giving is subtraction. In the spiritual realm, it is addition through obedience.

Greed and fear thrive in closed hands. They convince us that we must protect every dollar, control every outcome, and trust in our efforts. Giving disrupts that mindset. It opens your hands, and in doing so, it opens your life. You create space. You make room for more provision, clarity, divine partnerships, and unexpected blessings.

This is a truth confirmed by Scripture and by life itself. The person who sows generously will reap generously. It is not a matter of if, but when and how. Sometimes the return comes financially. At other times, it arrives in the form of peace, opportunities, relationships, or favour. God decides the form, but He never forgets the seed.

When you begin to operate from this posture of open-handed giving, you align yourself with a higher financial ecosystem. In this system, increase is not based on manipulation or competition. It flows through trust and obedience. You understand that the true measure of your wealth is not what you keep, but what you can give and still have peace. You stop giving out of pressure and start giving out of vision.

There is also a practical ripple effect. Giving creates healthier communities. It empowers people. It restores dignity. It meets needs that systems cannot reach. When you give to your church, your offering becomes part of the solution for someone's healing or hope. When you support a student, your generosity becomes the ladder that lifts another generation. When you bless a neighbour, you reinforce the kind of society where people look out for one another.

These acts may seem small, but they multiply. A single gift can change the direction of a household. A seed sown in love can lead to generational transformation. In this way, giving is not a loss. It is a legacy. It is a way of anchoring your influence in places your physical presence may never reach.

This is the cycle that God designed: one of trust, obedience, release, and return. You give from what you have, and in doing so, you activate the principle of increase. Not because you earned it, but because you honoured the One who gave you the seed in the first place.

The more you give, the more you grow. The more you release, the more you receive. And in time, you do not just witness the increase. You become an increase in the lives of others.

Forms of Giving

Giving is not limited to finances. Some of the most impactful forms of generosity are expressed in ways that cannot be measured in dollars. When we expand our understanding of giving, we begin to see opportunities to serve and bless others in every season of life, whether we have much or little to give.

True generosity is a lifestyle. It is the continual practice of offering what we have, wherever we are, for the benefit of others and the glory of God.

Here are some of the most powerful and practical forms of giving:

Time

Time is one of the most valuable gifts you can offer. In a world filled with hurry and distraction, your undivided presence can become a healing force. Volunteering at your church, mentoring a younger person in your field, helping a neighbour to run errands, or simply sitting with someone who is grieving, these moments speak volumes.

When you give your time, you give what cannot be refunded. And in doing so, you create bonds of trust, comfort, and shared purpose. Time given in love is never wasted.

Resources

We often overlook what we already have that could become someone else's breakthrough. Your closet, your pantry, your bookshelf, these hold items that could serve a student, clothe a family, or feed someone in need. Providing resources can also mean sharing tools, devices, or household items with someone who is starting over.

These acts of generosity send a powerful message: I see you, and I want to help. When we offer our resources freely, we turn everyday possessions into vessels of compassion.

Opportunity

This form of giving is often the most life-changing. Introducing someone to a job opening, writing a recommendation letter, sharing a platform, or connecting a person to your network can unlock doors that may have seemed permanently closed.

Opportunity is influence in action. It is one of the highest forms of generosity because it empowers others to stand on their own two feet. By giving opportunity, you multiply dignity, confidence, and long-term growth in others' lives.

Financial Giving

When it comes to money, giving should not be an afterthought. It should be intentional, prayerful, and built into your financial structure. One of the best ways to do this is by including giving as a dedicated line in your monthly budget. Just like rent, groceries, and savings, your giving deserves a place of priority.

Decide in advance how much of your income will consistently support tithing, charitable work, missions, or individual needs around you. This removes emotion from the decision and makes generosity a regular expression of your values.

Financial giving also invites discipline. It teaches you to give even when things are tight, knowing that provision flows through faith and stewardship, not fear. It reminds you that generosity is not just an act of overflow; it is often the seed that produces overflow.

Let your giving, whether in time, resources, opportunities, or finances, be consistent and joyful. Do not wait for the "perfect time" to give. Instead, make it a habit that flows naturally from who you are. When generosity becomes your way of life, you never run out of ways to bless others. And God, in His faithfulness, ensures that you never lack what you need.

Start Living Freely *NOW*!

Freedom is not a destination you stumble upon after everything in your life has been perfectly arranged. It is a mindset, a conviction, and a deliberate choice.

You do not wait for debts to disappear or investments to multiply before you begin living with clarity, peace, and purpose. If you keep postponing your peace until everything aligns externally, you may find yourself stuck in a cycle of waiting that never ends.

There will always be something that needs fixing. A bill to be paid. A goal yet to be reached. A savings account that still feels too small.

Freedom was never meant to begin at the finish line. It begins the moment you realign your priorities, redefine your values, and decide to trust God over circumstances. That is when you stop chasing the illusion of having it all together and start embracing the deeper reality that you are already enough in Christ.

You can walk in joy even when your goals are not yet complete. You can rest while your dreams are still in progress. True freedom is not delayed until your income reaches six figures or your retirement is fully funded. It is experienced when your identity and direction are no longer dictated by what you lack, but by what you believe.

When you release the idea that your external world must be perfect before you permit yourself to live fully, you take back your power. You begin to operate from alignment, not exhaustion. Your decisions become intentional, not reactive. You begin to say no without guilt, plan without panic, and give without fear.

This freedom is not loud or boastful. It is quiet, steady, and anchored. It shows up in how you manage your time, how you speak to yourself, and how you treat others. It is reflected in your ability to enjoy today, even as you plan for tomorrow.

Start now. Not when your loans are paid off or your account reaches a certain balance. Begin with what you have, where you are. Let peace be your starting point, not your reward. You will find that when your heart is free, your hands will begin to build more wisely.

Freedom in Mindset

Living freely begins in the mind long before it becomes evident in your bank account. It's a decision to shift your perspective, reframe your experiences, and trust that peace is cultivated through truth. These internal shifts lay the foundation for the kind of lasting freedom that no financial crisis can shake.

Letting go of comparison

Comparison is a silent thief of joy. When you measure your life against someone else's highlights, you end up feeling behind, even when you're exactly where God needs you to be.

Freedom means releasing the need to match others' pace or possessions. It means staying faithful to your path, trusting that your process is valid, and that progress, even when it looks different, is still progress.

Refusing to define your success by someone else's pace

Everyone's timeline is different. Some invest early. Others rebuild later in life. Some start businesses in their twenties. Others find purpose in their fifties. When you stop racing an invisible clock, you start living from a place of grace.

Success is not a sprint. It is a rhythm between stewardship, rest, obedience, and growth. Choosing your own pace is one of the most powerful forms of freedom.

Celebrating every small win along the way

You do not need to wait for a big breakthrough to rejoice. Every debt paid off, every budget followed, every moment you choose discipline over impulse is a win worth celebrating. These milestones are the building blocks that form financial stability. When you acknowledge them, you reinforce a mindset of gratitude. And gratitude unlocks contentment, one of the richest forms of wealth you can experience.

Choosing to speak life over your finances, even when you're still rebuilding

Words shape your atmosphere. Speaking defeat over your financial situation, even in jest, keeps you stuck in cycles of lack. Speaking life even when circumstances have not changed activates hope, sharpens focus, and attracts opportunities. Saying, "I'm learning to manage well," or "God is giving me wisdom for increase," trains your heart to expect better. That expectation fosters better habits and more favourable outcomes.

This kind of mental freedom transforms more than your money. It shapes your spirit. It changes how you show up at work with less stress and more purpose. It influences how you love your family more present and less preoccupied. It deepens how you invest your time more intentionally, less reactively. You stop performing and start living. You stop surviving and start building.

Freedom in mindset is the first step toward building wealth with peace and living with purpose, whether or not you have yet reached your financial goals.

A Legacy of Peace

True wealth is not defined by what you leave behind in your bank account. It is defined by the atmosphere you create, the values you model, and the peace that remains in the hearts of those you've touched.

The world is full of people chasing status and stacking assets, yet many live in unrest, uncertainty, anxiety, and disconnectedness. What the world truly needs is not more displays of affluence, but more people who are anchored, wise, and generous. People whose lives reflect wholeness from the inside out.

When you choose to live freely, generously, and with purpose, you begin to shape more than your financial future. You begin to model a way of living that invites others into a state of peace.

Children raised in a home where money is managed with wisdom and given with joy grow up with fewer financial fears. They learn to associate provision with trust in God, not pressure. They understand that wealth is not something to be hoarded but something to be stewarded for impact.

In your community, your freedom creates ripple effects. Instead of fostering competition, you foster collaboration. Instead of living with a scarcity mindset, you build circles of generosity. You share knowledge, offer opportunities, and support others without expecting anything in return. And through that posture, you inspire others to believe that a better way is possible.

Even after you are gone, the culture you built remains. Your financial discipline becomes the foundation upon which others build. Your giving becomes the story someone else talks about, how they were seen, supported, and strengthened. Your decisions today become part of a testimony that speaks long after your voice has faded.

That is what it means to leave a legacy of peace. It is not only about inheritance, but it is about influence. It's not only about money; it's about mindset. It is the quiet, consistent way you live your values, both in public and in private. And it is the gift you give to generations who will one day say, "Because they lived wisely and freely, I now know how to do the same."

> **Action Step:**
>
> Define what **financial freedom means to you** is it being debt-free, having a certain amount in savings, or having enough passive income to cover your expenses? **Write down three steps you can take right now** to move closer to that freedom. Then, **commit to giving whether it's time, resources, or money to help someone else without expecting anything in return.**

This kind of legacy is not built in a moment. It is built into daily choices. The choice to live below your means. The choice to give without grumbling. The choice to say no to unnecessary pressure and yes to purpose. The choice to trust God as your provider, not just your income as your source.

A legacy of peace is not only possible but also powerful. It begins with how you choose to live today.

Conclusion

Financial freedom is not a finish line. It is a posture of peace, purpose, and obedience that transforms how you view and use what you have, being anchored in what you have, regardless of its nature. When you stop letting money control your mood, your schedule, or your identity, you begin to live from a deeper well. A place where wisdom, generosity, and clarity lead the way.

> *True financial freedom is about having control over your life and using your wealth with purpose. The more you give, the more you grow. Wealth that isn't shared has no meaning. Start building a life where generosity and financial independence go hand in hand.*

In this chapter, you've seen that freedom begins in the mind and is sustained through intentional action. It's the decision to stop chasing wealth as a badge of success and start assigning it as a tool for a mission. It's the understanding that giving is not an interruption to your plans; it is part of God's divine system for increase.

And it's the willingness to redefine what it means to be rich: not by what you keep, but by what you give, build, and leave behind.

This is your invitation to live differently, guided by conviction. Not enslaved by bills and comparison but led by wisdom and grace. As you continue to grow in stewardship, remember that this freedom is not something for someday; it is now. The more you align your values with your finances, the more space you create for God to do exceedingly and abundantly beyond what you could ask or imagine.

Live wisely, give boldly and rest often. Also know this: the legacy you are building is not just about numbers. It is about the peace, purpose, and faith you leave in the hearts of others. You are not just earning, you are planting. And what you sow with faith and freedom will speak for generations to come.

You've now laid a firm foundation built on wisdom, discipline, and the kind of financial clarity that empowers you to live with both intention and peace. You've learned to generate income, manage money with purpose, and give from a place of overflow. But there is more. Financial wisdom doesn't stop at earning; it extends into the future, shaping generations you may never meet.

In the next section, we will step into the deeper call of stewardship: building a lasting legacy. Because true success is not just about what you accomplish in your lifetime, but about what continues to grow long after you're gone. If Part Three taught you how to live free, then Part Four will teach you how to leave something that lives on. Let's build with eternity in mind.

PART IV

LEGACY BUILDING AND LONG-TERM PLANNING

CHAPTER ELEVEN

SECURING YOUR FAMILY'S FUTURE

"A good man leaveth an inheritance to his children's children: and the wealth of the sinner is laid up for the just."

—Proverbs 13:22 (KJV)

There comes a time in every person's financial growth when the focus must shift from *"what am I building for myself"* to *"what am I leaving behind for others?"* True wealth is measured by how we prepare others to thrive with or without us. Securing your family's future is a demonstration of wisdom and spiritual responsibility.

Today, unexpected events can change everything in a moment; it has never been more vital to build systems that protect what you value most. Whether you are just starting out or already well on your financial path, the decisions you make now will echo into the lives of those you love. This chapter explores how to turn that intention into structure and how to ensure that your future blessings remain a source of peace, not pressure, for your family.

Why Estate Planning and Life Insurance Matter

When most people hear the words "estate planning," they imagine something reserved for the wealthy or elderly. Estate planning is for anyone who cares about what happens to their loved ones, their hard-earned assets, and their values after they are gone. It is one of the most profound ways to express love, protection, and responsibility. Life insurance, too, is often misunderstood as just a payout in the event of death. In reality, it serves as a financial shield and a strategic tool for legacy building and family stability.

The idea that we can leave something meaningful behind, not only in memory but in material support, is a biblical principle. Proverbs 13:22 reminds us that a good person doesn't merely live well, but prepares well, leaving an inheritance that reaches even their grandchildren. This is not about hoarding wealth. It is about creating continuity, safety, and opportunity.

As a financial educator and licensed agent in multiple five states namely, South Carolina, Texas, Michigan, Ohio, Minnesota, Tennessee, New York, and appointed by major corporations such as Transamerica, Nationwide, Pacific Life, Inherit Guard, and others, I often guide families through the critical steps of establishing wills, trusts, and affordable life insurance policies that protect them from financial catastrophe. Without such preparation, families are left to mourn under pressure, dealing not only with emotional loss but financial chaos, not to mention Probate Court challenges

My license allows me to help families build a strong financial foundation., I help individuals access tools and solutions tailored to their income level and life goals. Here are the major components we assist people in:

- Providing protection against market volatility, where their money can be moved from variable portfolios to indexed accounts.
- Show people have a guaranteed income for life
- How to have a tax-free account
- How to have probate court free accounts
- How to create generational wealth transfer
- Help people to customise an income replacement account
- How to set up children's financial plan
- We assess what fits best for each family, ensuring the protection they deserve, and we can match clients with the best value without bias.

In due course, estate planning and life insurance matter, because they speak for you when you are no longer here. They ensure your intentions are honoured and your family is cared for. In other words, it helps you distribute your assets instead of the government doing it for you.

How to Create Long-term Financial Security

Long-term financial security is not just about having money; it's about having a system in place that protects, multiplies, and sustains wealth through generations. This includes diversified income, protection strategies, emergency funds, and a clear financial blueprint that evolves as life changes.

1. Build Layers of Protection. Security starts with the right foundation. Emergency savings are crucial, but they are just the beginning. You need income protection through insurance, retirement accounts with tax advantages, and, where possible, investment accounts that grow with market trends. I provide education and tools to facilitate the setup of 401(k) rollovers, Roth IRAs, and annuities with long-term growth potential.

2. Plan for Life's Seasons. Financial security also means preparing for every stage of life, including raising children, buying a home, sending kids to college, and eventually retiring.

Each phase requires planning. It is wise to sit with someone who understands the full picture, not just your income, but your hopes, responsibilities, and legacy goals.

We don't offer one-size-fits-all solutions. We help families create a roadmap.

3. Teach Financial Literacy at Home. Creating security is not complete unless you pass on financial wisdom. Teach your children how money works, how to save, how to give, and how to invest. Invite them into your financial goals.

A legacy is not just built from assets; it is built from a mindset.

Reflection Question:

If something were to happen to me today, would my family be financially secure? Have I taken the right steps to protect them from financial hardship?

Steps To Financial Stability

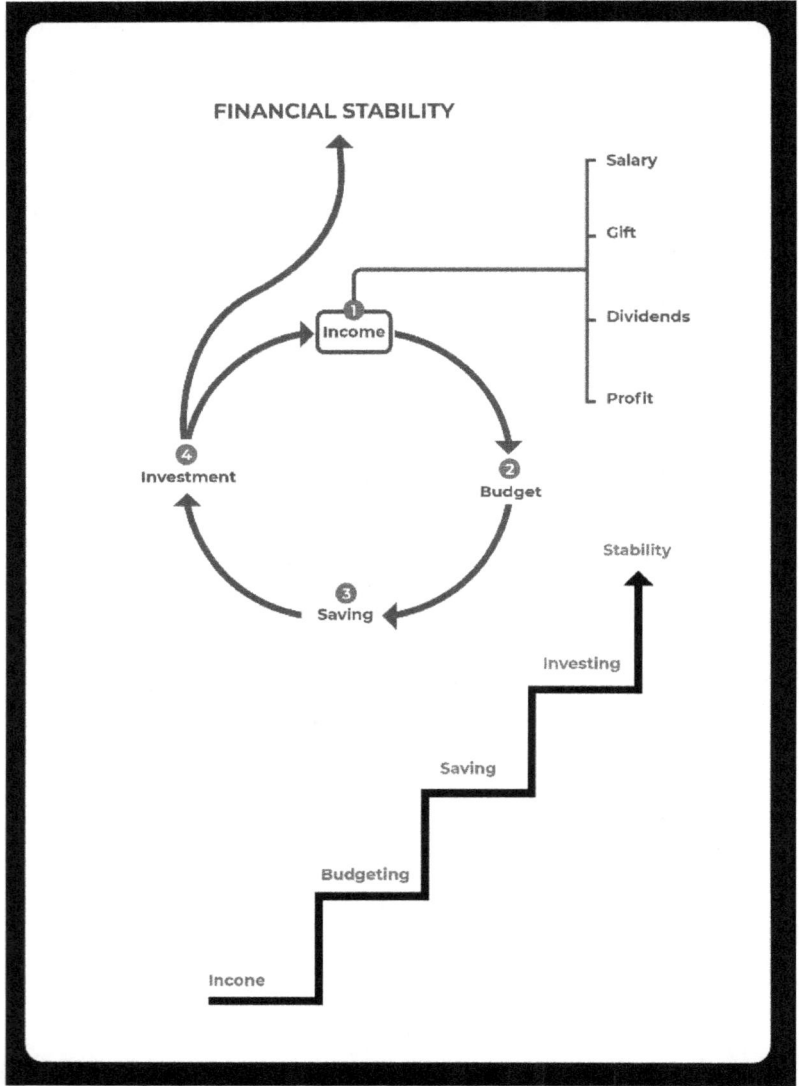

Figure 01: Steps to Financial Stability.

Start Protecting What Matters

No one plans to leave their family unprepared. Yet many people avoid conversations about death, inheritance, or incapacitation until it's too late. The most compassionate thing you can do is start these conversations now, while you still have the clarity and time to act.

1. *Identify What You Need to Protect.* Start by listing what matters: your children, your spouse, your ageing parents, your business, your home. Then ask: What will happen to these if I am not here? This mental exercise can help you prioritise protection.

2. *Get the Right Coverage,* as not all life insurance policies are the same. Some are temporary (term), others are permanent and come with living benefits. I help break down the jargon so families can make informed decisions. We match people with the kind of coverage that serves their goals now and in the future.

3. *Put Your Wishes in Writing.* Estate planning encompasses creating a will, appointing healthcare proxies, and establishing a trust, if applicable. These documents help eliminate confusion, conflict, and court battles. The earlier you do this, the more peace you give your family.

Protection is not just a financial task. It is spiritual stewardship. It is preparing your household for anything, so they can continue to thrive even if you are no longer present.

Your Legacy Starts TODAY!

Too many people postpone legacy conversations until retirement, or worse, until it's too late. Your legacy is not something you create at the end. It starts with the values you model, the decisions you make, and the protections you put in place today.

Legacy is about stewardship, not status. It is about how well you use what God has entrusted to you. You don't have to be a millionaire to leave something meaningful. You need to be intentional. Legacy includes the lessons you teach, the generosity you show, and the systems you build that last beyond your lifetime.

The families I serve come from diverse backgrounds: immigrants, single parents, couples in their prime, and retirees. They all share one thing in common: they want to make sure their loved ones are not left guessing. They want clarity, peace, and protection. That is what legacy looks like.

So, start now. Secure what matters. Speak blessings over your family through preparation. And remember, the best inheritance is not only in dollars, but also in discipline, wisdom, and foresight.

Your legacy begins with one decision: to take your future seriously today.

> **Action Step:**
>
> Review your **current financial protection plans. Do** you have an **emergency fund, life insurance, or a will** in place? If not, **take one action this week,** whether it's researching life insurance options, starting an emergency savings fund, or drafting a simple estate plan. **Protecting your family starts with one step today.**

Conclusion

Securing your family's future is not about predicting what will happen; it's about preparing with wisdom for whatever may come. It is a spiritual act, a practical responsibility, and an expression of love that speaks louder than words. Each decision you make today becomes a seed for peace, protection, and prosperity tomorrow.

As you've seen throughout this chapter, estate planning and life insurance are not luxuries reserved for a select few; they are tools every family can use to build stability.

> *Financial security for your loved ones isn't something to put off it's something to prioritize now. Don't leave your family's future to chance. The best gift you can give them is stability, protection, and a legacy that lasts beyond you.*

Financial security isn't built overnight, and legacy isn't measured by how much you leave behind, but by how intentionally you live right now.

Whether it's setting up the right insurance coverage, creating a will, or simply having a conversation with your loved ones, your preparation sets the tone for generations.

Let this chapter be your reminder that legacy is not for later; it is a living message. One of wisdom, provision, and honour. You have the power to shape your family's future. Do it prayerfully. Do it wisely. And do it now!

CHAPTER TWELVE

RAISING MONEY-SMART CHILDREN

"Start children off on the way they should go, and even when they are old, they will not turn from it."

—Proverbs 22:6 (NIV)

Money habits don't begin in adulthood; they are shaped in the earliest years of life. Every family has an opportunity to instil values that will guide children long after they leave home. Teaching kids about money isn't just about dollars and cents; it's about equipping them with the mindset and skills to make wise choices in a world full of financial distractions.

Children learn what they live, and when they grow up in homes where money is treated with respect, purpose, and clarity, they are more likely to adopt those same principles. In this chapter, we explore how to raise children who are not just financially aware but financially confident and capable.

If Not You, Someone Else Will

Children absorb information quickly, and if financial literacy isn't taught intentionally at home, they will adopt beliefs and habits from whatever source speaks the loudest. In the absence of consistent guidance, social media, television, video games, and peer groups become their financial instructors.

Unfortunately, these voices often promote shallow values, instant gratification, overspending, glorified debt, and financial risk without responsibility. Children are taught to value appearances over substance and consumption over contribution. Without proper context, money becomes a symbol of identity rather than a tool for purpose.

It becomes the sacred responsibility of parents and guardians to be the first and most trusted financial teachers. Teaching children about money isn't just about arithmetic or budgeting; it's about shaping their beliefs, their confidence, and their sense of stewardship. A child who is taught that money has purpose will grow up to handle it with clarity.

Financial education should begin early, long before a child receives their first paycheck or credit card offer. When a toddler receives a toy or snack, parents can use that moment to teach about choice, value, and patience. When a child envies what others have, it becomes an opportunity to teach contentment and prioritise values. These small conversations lay the foundation for a life of financial clarity and maturity.

Children are impressionable, but they're also incredibly capable. When we invest the time to explain why we save, why we wait, and why we give, we equip them with tools that will shape how they spend, save, and give as adults. And the earlier those seeds are planted, the deeper their roots will grow.

Other Influences That Shape Financial Beliefs

While parents play the most influential role in shaping a child's financial mindset, children also absorb cues from many other environments. Schools may introduce basic money concepts through math or economics classes, but they rarely offer in-depth, values-based financial education. Community centres, youth programs, or even religious institutions can provide supplementary guidance, but their effectiveness often depends on consistency and reinforcement at home.

The media is one of the most powerful teachers. Television shows, movies, music, and especially social media channels flood young minds with messages about money, wealth, and success. Influencers, celebrities, and advertisements often equate money with identity, fame, or happiness, shaping how children perceive success.

Without a counterbalance, these sources can misguide a child's aspirations and priorities.

Peers also influence financial behaviour more than many adults realise. Whether it's comparing clothes, gadgets, or allowances, children begin to assess their worth based on what they have or lack. These subtle social pressures can create feelings of inadequacy or entitlement, often long before a child understands how money is earned or managed.

Because of this, intentionality from parents and mentors becomes essential. If a child doesn't hear about financial values from trusted adults, they will adopt whatever lessons are most emotionally compelling or culturally dominant, even if they're misleading or harmful.

Money Lessons Begin at Home

Financial wisdom is first observed, not instructed. Children learn more by watching how we treat money than by what we say about it. When they see us budgeting, planning for expenses, saving for future goals, and giving consistently, they internalise those behaviours as normal. Home becomes their first financial classroom, and every transaction, no matter how small, can become a teachable moment.

For example, involving children in age-appropriate financial decisions, such as grocery shopping, comparing prices, or saving up for a desired toy, teaches them the concepts of planning and prioritisation. Showing them how you set financial goals for the family, whether it's saving for a vacation or cutting back on spending for a long-term objective, gives them a concrete sense of how discipline connects to reward.

Talking openly about money also helps remove any mystery or fear around it. Let them hear you speak positively and intentionally about your financial goals. Explain why you're making a certain purchase or choosing to delay another. Let them ask questions and provide honest answers that are appropriate for their age and level of understanding. These consistent conversations gradually shape a confident and responsible approach to finances.

As they grow older, children can be gradually introduced to budgeting their own money, managing allowances, and even participating in youth savings programs. The goal is not to impose rigid rules, but to cultivate a financial mindset grounded in discipline, foresight, and generosity. The earlier they associate money with intentional living and value-based decisions, the stronger their financial foundation will be.

How Children Can Practice What They Learn

Learning about money must be paired with experience. Children retain more when they can put principles into practice. Here are simple, age-appropriate ways to reinforce financial lessons:

Use a Three-Jar System: Label jars as Give, Save, and Spend. Each time a child earns or receives money, help them allocate a portion into each jar. This teaches balance and purpose.

Give Them a Budget: For school shopping or holiday gifts, provide a set amount and let them make the decisions. This introduces the concept of trade-offs and priority-setting.

Involve Them in Family Budgeting: Not every detail, but sharing how you plan for groceries, outings, or vacations can help them understand the value of planning.

Encourage Saving for Goals: If they want a toy or gadget, create a savings chart with them to track their progress. Celebrate when they reach the goal to reinforce the reward of patience.

Make Giving a Habit: Let them choose a cause to support or participate in a family giving tradition. It builds empathy and generosity.

These practices are identity-shaping moments, not tasks. Children who are involved in the process are more confident and intentional with their financial decisions.

Here's a simple table that illustrates a weekly money practice for children using the "Give, Save, Spend" method, an easy and practical way for kids to learn money discipline from a young age:

Category	Description	Suggested Amount	Activity Example
Give	Set aside a portion to help others or give to a cause.	$ 1.00	Donate to a church fund or buy a gift for someone in need.
Save	Reserved for long-term goals or future needs.	$ 4.00	Save for a $40 toy or book and track your progress weekly.
Spend	Used for small personal or discretionary use.	$ 5.00	Buy a snack, toy, or small accessory of choice.

Table No.2: Weekly Allowance Practice Table
(Example for a 10-year-old receiving $10/week)

This structured example helps children:

- Visualise where their money is going.
- Practice discipline by sticking to pre-set categories.
- Experience freedom within boundaries, knowing they can enjoy spending while also being generous and forward-thinking.

Feel free to customise it according to your children's needs and learning program.

Reflection Questions:

- Am I equipping my children with the financial skills they need to thrive? Or am I leaving them to figure it out on their own?
- What kind of money habits am I passing down?

Teach Financial Responsibility Instead of Handouts

One of the biggest disservices we can do for our children is to provide financially without teaching responsibility. Providing for a child's needs is an act of love. Equipping them to meet their own needs in the future is a wise act.

Children raised in homes where money flows freely without any accountability often grow into adults who expect resources without effort or who feel entitled without understanding the concept of stewardship.

Teaching financial responsibility means moving beyond giving money for the sake of convenience. It means taking the time to show your child how to handle what they receive. Whether it's allowance, gift money, or rewards from achievements, every coin becomes a tool for training.

You are not just handing them currency; you are handing them an opportunity to grow in decision-making, self-discipline, and foresight.

When children understand that money has value and comes with responsibility, they start making different choices. They pause before spending, they think before asking, and they begin to connect effort with outcome.

These are not lessons that can be outsourced or picked up overnight. They are cultivated in everyday interactions, such as how you respond to their requests, how you guide them through choices, and how you involve them in financial decisions within the home.

Create boundaries. Don't feel pressured to meet every desire instantly. When children understand that money is earned and not just handed out, they become more discerning, grateful, and motivated.

A 2023 study by the Consumer Financial Protection Bureau found that children who earn money through tasks and receive financial guidance from parents demonstrate greater financial competence by the age of 18. It shows that responsibility builds capacity.

Love is not measured by how often we say yes; it is measured by how well we prepare our children to thrive in the world without us. And one of the greatest gifts we can offer is the confidence to handle money with wisdom, restraint, and generosity.

Responsibilities Over Rewards

Instead of giving money as a casual reward, connect it to purpose and effort. Assign age-appropriate responsibilities around the home and link them to agreed financial outcomes. This does not mean children should be paid for every chore; some duties should be done simply because they are part of the family. However, additional tasks or consistent efforts can be a great opportunity to introduce earnings.

The key is consistency and clarity. When a child understands what is expected of them, how their actions impact their rewards, and what they are responsible for managing, they begin to develop a financial mindset rooted in accountability. It teaches that money is not something to be begged for, but something to be earned, respected, and handled with thought.

Teaching Through Consequences

One of the most powerful teachers in financial life is consequence. If a child spends all their money too quickly and cannot afford something they want later, resist the urge to bail them out. Let them feel the discomfort of their choice. That moment becomes a more effective teacher than any lecture. As painful as it may be to watch, these safe, small lessons during childhood prevent much costlier mistakes in adulthood.

Also, show them how to adjust. Sit down with them, review where their money went, and guide them in setting a new plan or savings goal. These practices not only build discipline but teach the art of resilience, how to recover and realign after a setback.

Your Money Habits Become Theirs

Children rarely become what we tell them; they become what they consistently see. Financial habits are one of the most silently absorbed behaviours in a household. Whether it's how you talk about bills, react to unexpected expenses, approach shopping, or handle giving, your children are always watching. What you normalise in your home becomes the template they carry into their adulthood.

If you constantly stress over money, the children or your family members absorb anxiety. If you spend impulsively, they learn to chase instant gratification. If you speak negatively about budgeting or saving, they internalise that discipline is painful rather than empowering. On the other hand, if they witness thoughtful planning, peaceful generosity, and clear priorities, they begin to mimic those values without even being asked.

According to a 2022 report from the University of Cambridge, children start forming money habits by the age of seven. These early impressions shape their future decisions around saving, spending, and prioritising needs over wants. That means by the time they hit adolescence, their financial behaviour is already on a trajectory, either one of stewardship or struggle.

This is why your money habits matter far beyond your own financial goals. You are setting a standard for how your children will interact with money for decades to come. Even if you feel like you're still learning or correcting your missteps, being transparent about your process can be just as powerful as having everything figured out. Your willingness to talk openly about budgeting, sacrifices, or long-term goals teaches them that money is not taboo, it's something to be handled with intention and care.

Modelling Healthy Financial Rhythms

Make your financial practices visible and understandable. If you're budgeting for groceries, let your child see how you make trade-offs. If you're saving for a trip or a major purchase, include them in the planning. Show them the joy of reaching a goal after consistent effort, because they are family lessons, not adult tasks.

Even small routines, such as keeping receipts, comparing prices, using a shopping list, or checking your bank balance, can serve as valuable teaching moments. When children see financial tools being used with confidence and purpose, they become less intimidated by money matters and more prepared to take ownership when their time comes.

Normalise Financial Conversations

Silence around money can be just as harmful as mismanagement. In many households, finances are either a source of conflict or completely avoided. This leaves children with uncertainty, fear, or unrealistic expectations. By creating a home environment where money is discussed openly without fear or shame, you build their confidence and curiosity.

This doesn't mean sharing every detail or placing adult burdens on them. It simply means helping them understand that money is a part of life, one that can be managed wisely and peacefully. It can be as simple as saying, "We're saving up for something important," or "We're choosing not to buy that right now because we have other goals."

From Observation to Ownership

The ultimate goal is not just for your children to repeat your actions but to understand the reasons behind them. Why do you save? Why do you tithe or give? Why do you avoid certain debts or prioritise investments? These reasons are what transform surface habits into deep values.

When children understand the reasoning behind good financial behaviour, they begin to take ownership. They ask questions. They express interest in planning. They develop goals. And over time, they begin to act with clarity and confidence even when you're not watching.

Action Step:

Start **one money lesson** with your child this week, whether it's giving them a small allowance to manage, teaching them how to save for a goal, or explaining the difference between needs and wants. **Lead by example** by discussing financial decisions openly so they learn from your habits.

Conclusion

Raising money-smart children is more than just financial literacy; it's about stewardship, discipline, and legacy, shaping a generation that not only survives but also contributes to building healthier economic systems.

Children who grow up with a clear understanding of money also develop a clear understanding of responsibility, purpose, and freedom. They learn that wealth is not something to be flaunted, but something to be multiplied and used for good.

As parents, guardians, mentors, and leaders, we are called to plant seeds not of entitlement but of trustworthiness. That trust begins with modelling, then continues with teaching, and eventually shows up in how our children live. When we give them the tools to manage their money wisely, we are also giving them the tools to manage their time, talents, relationships, and vision.

> *Your children's financial future starts with what you teach them today. They don't need to learn about money the hard way gives them the tools, knowledge, and confidence to make smart financial choices for life.*

No age is too early to begin. No lesson is too small to matter. Whether it's teaching them how to save part of their allowance, letting them sit in on a budget discussion, or simply allowing them to witness your contentment and generosity, you are shaping their framework for life.

Children do not need perfect financial examples. They need present ones. And every intentional step you take today becomes part of the financial legacy they will carry into tomorrow.

CHAPTER THIRTEEN

BECOME A FINANCIAL MENTOR AND EDUCATOR

"A generous person will prosper; whoever refreshes others will be refreshed."

—Proverbs 11:25 (NIV)

Financial mentorship is one of the most overlooked yet powerful ways to break the generational cycle of poverty. I have come to understand that true financial transformation is not complete until it is shared with others.

Many of us were never taught how money works; we had to learn through hardship, trial, and self-discovery. That's why I have made it my mission to ensure that others do not have to go through what I did to gain clarity.

In this chapter, I open the door for you to do the same. Whether you are a parent, a leader, a professional, or simply someone who has gained insight from this book, you are already qualified to make a difference. This is your invitation to teach what you now know, model what you now practice, and empower others with the truth that wealth is within reach when it is taught with compassion and lived with purpose.

Financial Literacy Should Be Shared, Not Kept

I have learned that financial literacy becomes more powerful when it is shared with others. Knowledge locked inside benefits no one.

As someone who was transformed through education, mentorship, and community, I now make it my mission to extend that same transformation to others. Teaching others about money is not a performance; it is a responsibility. When we hold financial wisdom within, we limit the growth potential of those around us.

Families thrive when financial knowledge circulates. Communities rise when informed individuals step forward and share. I believe this is how wealth becomes generational, not simply through inheritance, but through the teaching that precedes it. Sharing financial literacy doesn't require a title or a stage. It begins with one honest conversation, one lesson, or one answered question.

I encourage you to look around. Someone in your circle needs the clarity you've gained. A friend is confused about credit. A sibling needs help planning their budget. A church member is overwhelmed by debt. These are all mentorship opportunities. This book was written not only to educate you but to equip you to educate others.

Demonstrate Financial Principles to Family, Friends, & Community

Teaching financial principles begins with an example. What I model carries more weight than what I say. I consistently practice what I teach: saving before spending, paying myself first, giving with intention, and planning with foresight. These values show up in how I make decisions and how I handle setbacks.

Mentorship begins at home. My children watch how I handle grocery shopping, how I respond to financial stress, and how I celebrate wins. I don't hide the lessons. I let them see me budgeting. I involve them in giving. I share with them the purpose behind our spending. These practices leave a deeper imprint than lectures.

I also extend this example to my community. I offer workshops, lead discussions, and participate in programs that empower others with the tools to make wise financial decisions.

This is not about perfection. It is about consistency. I have seen neighbours, friends, and relatives grow financially, not because I told them what to do, but because I showed them what was possible.

Below is a simple demonstration guide anyone can adopt:

Area of Life	Demonstration Practice	Impact
Home	Involve children in meal budgeting	Builds awareness and value
Church	Tithe with transparency and purpose	It models stewardship and trust
Friendships	Discuss financial goals casually and respectfully	Encourage openness and learning
Community Events	Lead free budgeting or saving workshops.	Provides access and empowerment.

Table No.3: *Financial Principles to Family, Friends, and Community*

Reflection Questions:

⌘ Am I keeping my financial knowledge to myself, or am I helping others break free from financial struggles?

⌘ Who in my circle could benefit from what I've learned?

The Role of Faith-Based Financial Coaching

As a believer, I see financial coaching as a calling. Money management is not only a personal skill, but also a spiritual assignment. I approach financial coaching with reverence, understanding that I am helping others steward what God has entrusted to them.

Faith-based financial coaching brings a unique lens. It combines biblical principles with practical financial tools. It reinforces discipline, integrity, and trust in God's provision. I coach people to see giving as a kingdom act, saving as a form of obedience, and investing as a preparation for multiplication.

In my work as a licensed financial professional, I integrate these principles into every session, ensuring that my clients not only understand what to do with their money but also why they are making these decisions. Whether they are individuals, couples, or families, I take the time to align their financial goals with their values and faith.

The fruit of faith-based coaching is not just financial stability. It is peace of mind; it restores broken marriages. Legacy planning honours both God and family. And the most fulfilling part for me is seeing people experience freedom, not because they now have more money, but because they now have understanding.

Mentorship and Coaching for Financial Success

Becoming a financial mentor is not reserved for professionals. It is available to anyone willing to share, teach, and guide others with care and clarity. Through my journey, I have seen how mentorship opens doors. It breaks cycles of ignorance. It empowers entire households.

I invite you to consider joining this work. If you have found the information in these pages useful, then you already have what it takes to start guiding someone else. Whether through an agency or within your circle, there is room to lead. Financial mentorship is not about knowing everything; it is about being willing to learn with others, to ask the right questions, and to walk alongside them as they grow.

Mentorship begins with a conversation, a shared resource, or a common goal. From there, it grows into transformation. And I am here to support you. My work is designed not only to serve families but also to train new educators, mentors, and leaders in this financial space.

If you are ready to become a financial coach or educator, I invite you to connect with me. Let us build a community of wealth stewards who teach, train, and transform lives. Your experience matters. Your story matters. And your decision to lead could be the shift that someone else has been waiting for.

Get in Touch: Become a Financial Leader and Mentor

If this chapter has sparked a desire in you to mentor, teach, or grow as a financial leader, I would love to hear from you. Whether you're exploring coaching opportunities, looking to join our team, or need guidance on your next step, please fill out the form below, and I will personally follow up with you.

Name:

_____

Email Address:

_____

WhatsApp Number:

_____

City & State:

_____

Are you interested in:

☐ Learning how to become a financial coach

☐ Scheduling a one-on-one consultation

☐ Attending our financial mentorship webinar

☐ Learning more about joining our team

- ☐ Bringing financial literacy to your church or community
- ☐ Bringing financial literacy to your church or community
- ☐ Other:

_____
_____
_____
_____

Briefly share your interest or question:

_____
_____
_____
_____
_____
_____

How did you find this book?

- ☐ Referred by a friend
- ☐ Found online
- ☐ At an event or seminar

☐ Social media

☐ Other:

_____

_____

_____

_____

Preferred method of contact

☐ Email

☐ Phone call

☐ WhatsApp/Text message

Once completed, please send your responses as a picture to mgodiberthe@ymail.com.

Action Step:

Identify **one person in your family, workplace, or community** who could benefit from financial guidance. **Start a conversation** share a budgeting tip, recommend a financial book, or invite them to a financial literacy workshop. If you're ready, consider **mentoring someone or leading a small financial education session.**

Conclusion

True wealth multiplies when it is shared. The heart of mentorship is not expertise; it is willingness. Willingness to teach what you've learned, to model what you've mastered, and to encourage others who are just beginning their financial path. When you step into the role of a mentor or educator, you extend the impact of your knowledge far beyond your household.

Whether you guide one person or many, the seeds you sow through financial mentorship will bear fruit in generations to come. And you don't have to do it alone.

My work is to walk with you, support you, and empower you to step fully into your role as a steward and a teacher.

> *Financial wisdom isn't meant to be kept it's meant to be shared. By helping others grow in financial knowledge, you reinforce your discipline and multiply the impact. Teach, mentor, and empower, because true financial success includes lifting others.*

If you've felt the nudge to turn what you've learned into a tool for others, now is the time. Reach out. Join a network of financial leaders making a real difference. Let your life be a testimony of what is possible when knowledge is shared, purpose is clear, and generosity leads the way.

You are not just a reader; you are a builder of legacies. And it starts with how you choose to show up for others today.

CHAPTER FOURTEEN

TAKE CONTROL OF YOUR FINANCIAL FUTURE

"But remember the Lord your God, for it is He who gives you the ability to produce wealth, and so confirms His covenant, which He swore to your ancestors, as it is today."

—Deuteronomy 8:18 (NIV)

Taking control of your financial future means stepping into ownership of your life with both intention and faith. It is not enough to hope for stability or pray for abundance; action must follow conviction. The financial decisions we make today will either open or close doors for tomorrow.

That's why now, not someday, is the time to choose wisdom, to seek understanding, and to commit to strategies that secure our future. As someone who has walked this path, I know that financial freedom is not found in luck, but in clarity, planning, and mentorship. In this chapter, I'll show you how to move from passive living to purposeful wealth-building through informed protection, education, and legacy planning.

Explore the Right Financial Protection for You

Wealth is not simply about how much you accumulate; it is also about how well you protect what you've built. One of the most effective and overlooked pillars of financial security is protection planning. This includes life insurance, critical illness protection, long-term care, and other forms of coverage designed to ensure that your family is not left vulnerable in the face of unexpected events.

As a licensed professional in the financial industry, I educate families on how to review their protection plans carefully. Many people assume that workplace benefits are enough. Others avoid thinking about protection altogether because it feels uncomfortable. Yet ignoring this aspect of wealth leaves gaps that can destabilise an entire household.

Through our platform, we provide families with access to top-rated insurance providers and help them compare options to suit their specific needs. From term insurance to permanent solutions, from individual to family coverage, protection is a proactive decision, not a reactive one.

Protection is not just about death; it's about living with peace of mind. It is about knowing that your children can continue their education, your mortgage will not become a burden, and your legacy will not be disrupted by crisis.

When considering the right financial protection for yourself and your family, it's important to understand that this step is not reserved for the wealthy or those approaching retirement. It is a necessary part of every stage in life. Financial protection is about creating a strong foundation that shields your loved ones and your income against unforeseen events.

Whether you're just starting your career, raising a family, or entering your later years, there are tools and strategies available in the United States that can provide coverage and peace of mind. Below are some of the most essential financial protection options every individual and household should consider:

1. Life Insurance

Term Life Insurance: Provides coverage for a specific period (e.g. 10, 20, 30 years). It is generally more affordable and suitable for income replacement.

Whole Life Insurance: Permanent coverage with a cash value component. Premiums remain level.

Universal Life Insurance: Flexible permanent coverage with adjustable premiums and death benefits.

Indexed Universal Life (IUL): Links cash value growth to a stock market index. Offers protection with upside potential and limited downside risk.

2. Disability Insurance

Replaces a portion of income if you're unable to work due to illness or injury. Can be short-term or long-term.

Often underused, despite the high likelihood of needing it during a working lifetime.

3. Critical Illness Insurance

Offers a lump-sum payout upon diagnosis of serious illnesses like cancer, heart attack, or stroke.

Helps cover out-of-pocket medical expenses or loss of income during treatment.

4. Long-Term Care Insurance

Covers the cost of care if you need assistance with daily activities (e.g., bathing, dressing) due to ageing, chronic illness, or disability.

Can be standalone or added as a rider to a life insurance policy.

5. Health Insurance

While often employer-provided, families and individuals can buy private or ACA marketplace plans.

Vital for protecting against overwhelming medical costs.

6. Umbrella Insurance

Provides additional liability coverage beyond the limits of homeowners, auto, or boat insurance.

Protects your assets from major claims or lawsuits.

7. Legal Tools for Estate Protection

Wills and Trusts: Direct how your assets should be distributed.

Power of Attorney & Health Care Proxy: Assign decision-making authority if you become incapacitated.

Beneficiary Designations: Ensure life insurance and retirement accounts pass to intended individuals.8. Emergency Fund (Financial Buffer)

Though not an insurance product, it protects against unexpected short-term disruptions like job loss or medical bills.

Join Our Financial Literacy Training Program

Knowledge is the foundation of transformation. This book is a powerful start, but lasting change requires consistent learning and structured mentorship. That is why I invite you to participate in our Financial Literacy Training Program. This is where concepts become clear and plans become action.

Our program is designed for individuals, couples, and families who are ready to build real wealth with understanding. Whether you're starting from scratch, recovering from financial mistakes, or simply seeking to expand your impact, this program provides practical tools, expert insights, and ongoing support.

We walk you through key areas including budgeting, protection, saving and investing, retirement planning, and income strategies. We use proven systems and customised coaching to help you build not only wealth but confidence. As you learn, you also have the opportunity to teach others, expanding your impact and opening the door to a professional income stream should you choose to become licensed in the industry.

What makes our program exceptional is its model, which empowers individuals not only to learn but also to earn, teach, and lead. Unlike traditional financial institutions that offer only their proprietary products, you will gain access to a wide marketplace of options. This ensures that recommendations are based on suitability, not sales quotas. Through this platform, we can:

Offer diverse financial products from multiple top-rated providers, ensuring families receive the best-fit solution for their needs rather than a one-size-fits-all plan.

These offerings include:

- Life insurance

Many companies offers term life, whole life, and indexed universal life (IUL) through top carriers. The key difference is education. Clients are taught the purpose of each type of insurance and how to align it with their income level, age, health, and legacy goals.

Some policies include living benefits, which allow access to the death benefit in the event of a critical illness or other specified events.

- Retirement accounts

Options like Traditional IRAs, Roth IRAs, SEP IRAs, and 401(k) rollovers are provided. We emphasises retirement planning with tax strategy, ensuring clients know the difference between taxable, tax-deferred, and tax-free income in retirement.

- Living benefits

Offered through life insurance policies, these benefits enable clients to receive a portion of the policy's value while still alive if diagnosed with a chronic, critical, or terminal illness. This option is rarely explained in employer-based plans, yet it is our major focus.

- College savings plans

Rather than promoting only 529 plans, we also discuss alternative education savings options, such as cash value life insurance strategies and UGMA/UTMA custodial accounts, which may offer more flexibility and control.

⌘ Annuities

We work with providers that offer fixed, indexed, and variable annuities, focusing on income guarantees, principal protection, and growth opportunities without market risk, depending on the product. Clients are guided through suitability based on age, goals, and risk tolerance.

⌘ Mutual funds

Available through affiliated partners, mutual funds are introduced with a clear understanding of fees, fund types, and performance history, and are often packaged in IRAs or college plans. Unlike some retail settings, the goal is not to sell but to strategize.

⌘ Long-term care solutions

We provides hybrid products that combine life insurance with long-term care benefits, ensuring clients don't "lose" their premiums if long-term care is not used. This differs from standalone LTC policies, which are often "use-it-or-lose-it."

⌘ Debt management services

Through vetted partners, clients receive personalised debt payoff strategies using snowball or avalanche methods, debt consolidation, and credit education. Our company doesn't act as a collection agent, but rather as a financial coach.

⌘ Tax-advantaged savings tools

This includes Roth IRAs, IULs, and annuities structured to reduce tax liability. Clients are taught about the three tax buckets (taxable, tax-deferred, and tax-free) and how to allocate their income wisely for retirement efficiency.

These products offer families a range of tailored options, alleviating the pressure to conform to a single product line and instead focusing on what truly aligns with their financial goals.

Reflection Questions:

⌘ Am I actively shaping my financial future?

⌘ Or am I waiting for things to change on their own?

⌘ What is stopping me from making bold financial decisions today?

Attend Live Events and Financial Workshops

We grow best in environments that challenge and empower us. Live events and workshops are a vital part of personal development, especially when it comes to financial growth. These gatherings provide community, accountability, and exposure to new tools and strategies that can elevate your mindset and methods.

Our events feature real stories, expert panels, guest speakers, and hands-on training. You learn how others have overcome debt, built businesses, protected their families, and achieved their goals. You connect with mentors, build relationships with like-minded individuals, and receive practical assignments to apply what you've learned.

Workshops also allow you to experience firsthand how financial education can become a movement in your community. You may find yourself inviting others, leading small groups, or launching your financial workshops with our guidance and support. These are not just events; they are platforms for activation.

Sustain Wealth Beyond a Lifetime

The final step in taking control of your financial future is preparing for a lifetime beyond your own. This involves estate planning, wealth transfer strategies, and clear communication about your financial wishes and goals. It is not enough to build wealth; you must preserve it.

Too often, families lose everything in a single generation due to a lack of planning. Documents are not in order, beneficiaries are not up to date, taxes are not considered, or assets are not adequately protected. All of these oversights can be avoided with intentional preparation.

I help families create estate plans, trusts, wills, and other tools that enable them to pass on their assets in a structured and tax-efficient manner. We believe that legacy is more than what you leave behind; it is how well you prepare others to carry it forward.

Taking control means not only preparing for your retirement but also preparing your family to live out your values, uphold your vision, and continue your financial legacy with confidence. When your money has direction beyond your life, your influence never ends.

Action Step:

Commit to your financial growth by taking one concrete action today. Whether it's inquiring about an insurance policy, enrolling in a financial training program, signing up for mentorship, or attending a financial literacy event, take the next step. Your financial transformation starts with action.

Conclusion

There is no better time than now to take full control of your financial future. The tools, knowledge, and mentorship are within your reach; you only need to make the decision.

From protecting your family today to building a lasting legacy for generations, every step matters. If anything, you've read in this book has stirred questions, sparked ideas, or clarified your next steps, I encourage you to act.

Please revisit Chapter 13 and fill out the Financial Mentorship Form provided. Once complete, please email it to the listed address, so we can begin a conversation. I am here to walk with you, offer guidance, and equip you to rise because your financial destiny is too important to leave to chance.

> *Your financial future is in your hands; no one else will build it for you. The longer you wait, the longer you stay stuck. Make the decision today to invest in yourself, seek expert guidance, and take control of your future. The future you dream of is possible, but only if you take action now.*

CONCLUSION

YOUR NEXT STEP TO MAKING SMART-MONEY CHOICES

Congratulations on reaching this point, as you read *Smart-Money Faithful Living: Strategies for Financial Security and Success*. You have taken an important step toward taking control of your financial future.

The next step is to commit to the habits and strategies that will lead you to long-term financial stability and independence. Financial growth is an ongoing process of learning, discipline, and action. The principles and strategies you have explored in these pages are just the beginning of what is possible when you take ownership of your financial decisions and apply them with consistency.

Now, I invite you to take the next step by engaging further with the financial literacy, mentorship, and coaching opportunities available. Through my training programs, financial workshops, and one-on-one coaching, you will gain deeper insights, practical tools, and personalised support to help you make smart money choices that lead to lasting financial security.

These programs are designed to provide you with the accountability, education, and mentorship necessary to apply these financial principles in your daily life and achieve measurable results.

By joining my financial training program, you will:

- ✓ Gain expert guidance on budgeting, saving, debt management, investing, and wealth-building strategies.
- ✓ Receive personalised mentorship to help you overcome financial challenges and create a clear, actionable plan for your future.
- ✓ Join a community of like-minded individuals committed to financial growth and security.
- ✓ Learn how to protect your wealth through insurance, estate planning, and legacy-building strategies.
- ✓ Use the accompanying resources and workbook exercises to reinforce and apply what you've learned in a meaningful way.

If you're ready to take full control of your finances, build wealth with purpose, and create a secure and independent financial future, this is your opportunity.

Don't let this moment pass. Commit to becoming financially empowered today.

Please take the next step now, enrol in my financial literacy training program, schedule a mentorship session, or inquire about personalised financial coaching.

I look forward to guiding you through this transformative experience and helping you achieve the financial confidence and success you deserve. Your financial future is in your hands. Let's take this step together.

FINANCIAL COACHING & TRAINING ENROLMENT FORM

I appreciate your interest in my financial literacy training program and mentorship! Please complete the form below and email a copy to mgodiberthe@ymail.com to receive a complimentary financial consultation.

Personal Information:

Full Name:

_____

Email Address:

_____

WhatsApp Number:

_____

Preferred Contact Method (Email/Phone):

_____

Your Financial Journey:

Which areas of financial growth are you most interested in?

☐ Budgeting and Money Management

☐ Saving and Emergency Planning

- ☐ Debt Reduction Strategies
- ☐ Investing and Wealth Building
- ☐ Insurance and Financial Protection
- ☐ Legacy Planning and Estate Management

What inspired you to take this step toward financial literacy and stability?

_____

_____

_____

_____

_____

_____

_____

What are your biggest financial challenges or goals?

_____

_____

_____

_____

_____

_____

_____

_____

Have you ever participated in a financial education program before? (Yes/No) If yes, please specify.

_____

_____

_____

_____

_____

On a scale of 1-10, how committed are you to improving your financial future?

_____

Next Steps:

Once you submit your details, my team will contact you with more information about the program and guide you through the enrolment process.

Let's Begin This Incredible Transformation Together!

ABOUT THE AUTHOR

Godiberthe Mutayisebya is a dedicated and compassionate Licensed Financial Professional committed to educating families and small businesses on building strong financial foundations in preparation for a self-sufficient retirement.

Born in Kayove, Western Province, Rwanda, Godi is the third child of Mwalimu Gerard Munyankunge, a schoolteacher, and Winifrida Mukantagara, a farmer. Her love for education, inherited from a family of educators that included her grandfather, father, paternal aunt, and older sister, was evident from an early age. Despite facing challenges, she completed her elementary education with passion and aspired to attend secondary school in prestigious public or religious institutions. Although she did not initially receive that opportunity, her family, believing in her potential, supported her education at a private school for seven years despite the heavy financial burden.

Although her dream was not to become a teacher, she earned a diploma in education and taught 7th grade at Ecole Primaire de Remera. Due to regional instability, she left the country. She pursued higher education abroad, obtaining a Bachelor's degree in Business Administration with a major in Economics and a Master's degree in Agribusiness Management. With a desire to change her career path, her first job after graduating was as an instructor in the Business Administration department at Adventist University Zurcher in Madagascar. She taught with passion and eventually became the founder and owner of a kindergarten school.

Teaching seemed to be her calling. She homeschooled her children, tutored friends' children, and took on substitute teaching assignments in elementary and middle schools. As her father wisely said, "Teaching is a noble task; if you want many friends, be a teacher. If you want enemies, be a teacher too. It's up to you to choose." This rich background led her to continue and commit to improving financial literacy for adults, families, and small businesses.

Beyond teaching, Godi has served in various capacities, including church treasurer, accountant for ADRA International projects in Madagascar, Water Mission International in Sri Lanka, Donor Care Specialist for Water Mission in the USA, Patient Care Technician in hospitals and nursing homes, Cashier and Customer Care representative at Lowe's Home Improvement, and Mail Carrier for USPS. She serves as a State Notary Public in her community.

Her love for teaching, telling stories, sharing knowledge, and preparing herself and others for challenging times, coupled with her empathy and integrity, are qualities she attributes to her mother. "I owe it to my MOTHER," she proudly adds.

Godiberthe's debut book, *Smart Financial Choices,* in 2024, offers practical wisdom and heartfelt guidance for managing money with intelligence and intention. Designed to be both accessible and transformative, the book equips readers, particularly parents and young professionals, with strategies to establish healthy financial habits from the ground up.

Rooted in real-life experience and compassionate insight, Godi's writing reveals how smart financial choices can cultivate lifelong abundance and stability, leaving a lasting footprint of generational wealth and well-being.

Contact Godiberthe Here:

Web: www.mutayisebya.wealthfootprints.com

https://agents.worldfinancialgroup.com/Godiberthe-Mutayisebya- 92LQT

Email: mgodiberthe@ymail.com

YouTube: @Godiberthe Mutayisebya

Follow me on Facebook & Instagram:

@Godiberthe Mutayisebya

www.ingramcontent.com/pod-product-compliance
Lightning Source LLC
Chambersburg PA
CBHW070531090426
42735CB00013B/2938